ENTERTAIN LIKE A GENTLEMAN

David Harap

New Year Publishing LLC
Danville, California

Entertain Like a Gentleman

Copyright ©2011

orders@newyearpublishing.com
http://www.newyearpublishing.com

ISBN 978-1-935547-19-8 (Trade Hardcover)
ISBN 978-1-935547-18-1 (Trade Paperback)
Texas Edition ISBN 978-1-935547-20-4

Cover design by Jeff Weeks
Interior design and layout by Val Sherer, Personalized Publishing Services

All rights reserved. No part of this book may be used or reproduced in any manner whatsoever without the written permission by the author, except in the case of brief quotations embodied in critical articles and reviews. Illustrations may not be copied or used or reproduced in any manner whatsoever without the written permission of the author.
Printed in the USA.

New Year Publishing, LLC
144 Diablo Ranch Court, Danville, CA 94506 USA

acknowledgments

THERE ARE SO MANY PEOPLE that I am grateful to for their amazing friendship and support over the years, listing all of them by name would take too many pages.

My publisher, Dave Morris offered his boundless encouragement and generosity, which allowed this book to become a reality. What started as innocent banter with him over too many drinks in Dubai has become the book you now hold in your hands.

Central Market and their cooking school took a leap of faith in allowing me to start teaching classes. That ignited my passion for teaching about cooking and showing others how to have more fun in the kitchen.

To an individual who shall not be named but was my inspiration for many of these recipes, thank you. She acted as a sounding board and muse for much of the creative process.

Bruce and others graciously lent their time to help proofread the draft.

JJ McLaughlin, a talented Austin-based writer who helped add a creative spike to the book.

My parents, who always encouraged me to follow my passions.

Finally, I thank the countless friends who were willing culinary guinea pigs during the recipe testing process.

Contents

ENTERTAINING 101 2
    a gentleman's 25 tenets for stress free entertaining 3
    basic tools for a well equipped kitchen 6
    measure equivalents and metric conversions 9
    what and how much do i need? 10
    top 10 assumptions for all of the recipes 12

SCOTCH TASTING AFFAIR 14
    walnut chutney 17
    duck prosciutto with walnut chutney 18
    smoked trout rillettes 20
    risotto scotch eggs 24
    dark chocolate tart with pretzel crust 26

SUPER BOWL/MARCH MADNESS 30

- tomatillo guacamole salsa 32
- edamame dip 33
- pork, pork, pork and sauerkraut stew 34
- bison lollipops in dried cherry sauce 36
- turkey sliders with chipotle thousand island dressing 38
- italian macaroni pie 40
- "jambalaya" bread pudding 42
- sweet potato salad with mustard greens and bacon vinaigrette . 45
- sinful vanilla bourbon rice pudding 46

CHEESE AND WINE PARTY 50

- paprika candied pecans 53
- garlic and thyme marinated warmed olives 54
- dates stuffed with blue cheese mousse 55
- parmesan crisps with goat cheese and chive mousse 56
- savory jam elephant ears (palmiers) 58
- tarragon chicken skewers with pistachio cream sauce 60
- balsamic chocolate truffles 62

THE INITIAL FLAME. 66

- pancetta wrapped shrimp with mustard wasabi dipping sauce . 69
- goat cheese quesadillas with watermelon salsa 70
- sake and miso marinated skirt steak salad 72
- grilled fruit and pound cake napoleon with berry sauce and tequila whipped cream 74

POOL PARTY 78
    cold melon soup shooters with prosciutto salt 80
    drunken pineapple rum shrimp ceviche 82
    cobb salad sandwiches 84
    lamb sliders with mint yogurt sauce and homemade
    pickled onions 86

TAILGATING IN STYLE 90
    grilled vegetable antipasto with goat cheese on crostini . . . 92
    chili rubbed beef tenderloin sliders with cilantro lime mayo . . 94
    roasted corn salad 96
    s'mores bars 97

OCTOBERFEST 100
    homemade bratwurst patty sandwiches on pretzel rolls . . . 102
    bratkartolffen (fried potatoes laced with bacon and onions) . . 105
    schnitzel with baked apples stuffed with spicy red cabbage . . 106
    apple gingerbread bread pudding 110
    gingerbread 110

COOKING WITH KIDDOS 114
    dinosaur eggs 116
    super crunchy fish sticks 117
    mac 'n cheese 118
    violet's chocolate pudding 120

10 DOUBLE DATE NIGHT 122

brie en croute and spinach salad *124*
olive oil poached halibut with mint lemon pesto *126*
fennel and spinach strudel *128*
pomegranate semifreddo with chocolate sauce *130*

11 ROMANTIC DINNER (SPRING/SUMMER) 134

beet grapefruit salad *136*
chicken piperade over wasabi cauliflower puree *138*
haricot verts with tarragon butter and black sesame seeds . . *140*
white chocolate ginger mousse *141*

12 ROMANTIC DINNER ANOTHER NIGHT (FALL/WINTER) . 144

farmers' market grilled chopped salad with blood orange vinaigrette *146*
syrah braised and grilled short ribs on a bed of mascarpone jalapeño polenta *148*
pomegranate glazed carrots *150*
poached pears with dark chocolate sauce *151*

13 BREAKFAST IN BED 154

brioche french toast stuffed with strawberries & cream . . . *157*
ginger scones with peach bellini jam *158*
low fat granola parfait *160*

14 BRUNCH WITH THE IN-LAWS 164

    pumpkin muffins with brown sugar creme filling 166
    baked eggs with gruyere in prosciutto cups 168
    peaches in vanilla syrup over cinnamon yogurt 170

15 COCKTAIL PARTY FINGER FOOD 174

    ginger scallops on wonton crisps with candied jalapeño . . . 177
    crispy olives stuffed with chicken & feta sausage 178
    chipotle marshmallow crispy treats 179
    miniature crab corn cakes with chive caper sauce 180
    salmon in blankets with fried serrano cream 182
    sweet potato, ham and leek frittata wedges with lemon aioli . 184
    tomato skewers with tequila vinaigrette 186
    walnut, arugula and blue cheese crostini 188
    white chocolate spice cookies 190
    rum balls 192

16 POKER NIGHT WITH THE BOYS 196

    duck confit jalapeño poppers 198
    pumpkin seed crusted chicken bites with chipotle yogurt
    dipping sauce 200
    texas chili 202
    winners buttermilk pie 204

SHOPPING LIST INDEX	*207*
ABOUT THE AUTHOR	*237*
ORDER FORM	*239*

ENTERTAIN LIKE A GENTLEMAN

David Harap

ENTERTAINING 101

... A gentleman's 25 tenets for stress free entertaining

... Basic tools for a well equipped kitchen

... Measure equivalents and metric conversions

... What and how much do I need?

... Top 10 assumptions for all of the recipes

a gentleman's 25 tenets for stress free entertaining

1. You have to plan. A football coach does not go into game day without a plan and you shouldn't have guests over without a game plan.

2. Don't be shy about asking if your guests have any dietary restrictions. It is polite to have food options to accommodate allergies, religious restrictions, etc.

3. If you are entertaining a romantic interest, it is wise to learn what she likes and be fascinated by her current diet (while constantly reminding her that she looks great just the way she is).

4. Develop a schedule for shopping and cooking. Most of these recipes can be partially or fully prepared in advance. Develop a timeline of what needs to get done and when.

5. Don't invite more people than you can handle. If you are hosting a Super Bowl party or a wine tasting, it is fine to have a few more guest than chairs. Standing helps facilitate mingling.

6. Plan your menu around dishes where most of the preparation is done in advance, like most of the recipes in this book. It is not a romantic dinner if you are sweating in the kitchen and your guest is sitting alone at the table.

7. Checklists are key! Shopping lists, to do lists and invite lists, etc. all let you feel that you have everything under control. I have a white board posted on the refrigerator door where I make a list of the agenda for the day.

8. Candlelight makes anybody look more attractive ... including you. Avoid long tapered candles on the table that can be an obstacle to conversation. A single candle in the bathroom is always a nice touch, for several reasons.

9. Clean as you go. Don't make guests feel like you're tidying up because the party's over. Instead, try to grab crumpled napkins and dirty plates every time you walk into the kitchen. Try not to leave a sink full of dirty dishes sitting around to the morning. DO NOT LET YOUR GUESTS HELP WITH THE DISHES!

10. Do not assume your guests will bring beverages or food unless it is called for in the invitation as part of a theme. Plan on having everything your guests will need to eat and drink. If your guests ask what they should bring, wine or dessert is always an acceptable option.

11. A few days before your event, clean your place! A dirty house or apartment sends an awful message to your guests and makes them question how sanitary the kitchen prep was. A woman will not spend the night if she is disgusted by your bathroom.

12. Clean out your refrigerator and freezer before you come home with 100 bags of groceries. Toss out anything you can no longer identify.

13. Take an inventory of your serving dishes. Don't waste valuable time on the day of the event trying to remember where you've stashed the platters or plate. For sit-down dinners, you can set the table ahead of time.

14. If you do not own enough serving platters and serving utensils, most party supply stores have inexpensive disposable platters and large spoons/forks that look good. Guests are going to be focused on the food, not the serving platters.

15. Spontaneity is fun, but not when it comes to hosting parties. You want to give your guests at least 2 weeks notice. This gives them time to put it on the calendars and reply, and you time to plan. Provide the date, time, theme and a map, in the invitation.

16. Have some food available for your guests to nibble on as soon as they arrive, it could be as simple as a cheese plate or nuts. They will probably have a drink or two before you serve dinner and you want them to have something to absorb the alcohol.

17. Do not forget about non-alcoholic beverages. Have plenty of bottled water, iced tea and soda. Be prepared to offer your guests coffee and decaffeinated tea at the end of the evening.

18. While not necessary, if you are going to use a tablecloth use inexpensive white tablecloths. This way you can bleach out any stains … and there will be stains!

19. Do a reality check – delete and diminish as needed. Delete anything that is going to put undue pressure on you (like inviting an ex) and simplify where you can (focus on dishes you can prepare in advance, or pick up a store bought dessert).

20. Dress comfortably but neat. If you are comfortable, you will put your guests at ease.

21. Keep the conversation focused on the guest, the wine…anything but yourself. Never talk about how much money you spent on the food or how much effort you put into the evening. You want to give the impression that you had fun (hopefully you did) and that it was effortless to arrange the party.

22. Find a good wine shop, supermarket, butcher, and fish monger and become friendly with the staff. Being able to rely on their expertise will make your life easier.

23. Be polite at all times and make every guest feel equally welcome. If you are not polite then you are not a gentleman, no exceptions!

24. 'Monday Morning Quarterback' after the party is over. Go back to your checklists and make notes of what you did well, what you'd like to do differently next time, and anything you overlooked. The next time you plan a dinner party you'll save time by not having to reinvent the wheel or making the same mistakes twice.

25. Above all, know yourself. Paying attention to the details is nice, but make sure you're not so focused on delivering perfection that the planning is exhausting. Entertaining should not keep you from relaxing and truly enjoying the company of your guests. They are the real reason for your party - so have fun!

basic tools for a well equipped kitchen

Play With Knives

Precision cutting takes practice – Don't assume all kitchen knives are created equally either. Japanese santoku knives are light, sharp, and totally utilitarian!

TIP: Improvisation works only with experience. Slowly cut thin strips.

big ticket items

FOOD PROCESSOR If you plan on entertaining even occasionally or for big crowds, this will make your life so much easier.

IMMERSION BLENDER if you are not ready to commit to a food processor, then an immersion blender is a great option. They are a fraction of the cost of a food processor and often have several attachments that can handle most of your needs. The only real drawback is that the attachments have a smaller capacity and you will have to perform steps in multiple batches.

A GOOD SIZE CUTTING BOARD (EITHER PLASTIC OR WOOD) You will spend more time working on the cutting board than any other surface so get the largest cutting board that will fit on your counter. Use white vinegar or a bleach dilution to clean your cutting board. Buy an empty spray bottle and fill it with diluted bleach, 1 tablespoon of bleach to 1 quart of water. Use that to clean and sanitize your cutting board every time you use it, especially after working with raw meat or fish.

CHEF'S KNIFE Buy one that feels good in your hand. They can range from 6 inches to 10 inches. A serrated knife is helpful to have as well. They are great for certain tasks like cutting bread and tomatoes. Don't waste your money on the large sets of knives. They include many unnecessary knives that will often only collect dust.

STURDY MIXING BOWLS A three-piece set that includes one big bowl is all you really need.

12-INCH SKILLET AND NON-STICK 10 INCH PAN A 12-inch cast iron skillet is an inexpensive and a great addition to any kitchen; it just takes a little TLC to maintain.

MEDIUM SAUCE PAN (1 TO 2 QUARTS)

LARGE SAUCE PAN (4 QUARTS OR LARGER)

MEASURING SCALE An inexpensive one is fine. It takes stress out of cooking not having to guess.

little ticket items

A QUALITY GRATER SUCH AS MICROPLANE You will reach for a grater more than you think: lemon/lime zest, cheese, nutmeg, etc. Freshly ground nutmeg makes a huge difference in any dish.

BLACK PEPPER THAT COMES WITH GRINDER ATTACHED They are cheap and available in every supermarket. If you even think of buying pre-ground pepper I will be tempted to track you down and smack you.

A GOOD CORKSCREW AND BOTTLE OPENER You probably already have those!

MEASURING SPOONS

A 2-CUP MEASURING CUP

WOODEN MIXING SPOONS

A PAIR OF BASIC TONGS

A BAKING SHEET

NON-STICK SILICONE PAD THAT FITS YOUR BAKING SHEET Silpat is the most common brand, but there are others out there. They make baking a breeze.

INSTANT-READ THERMOMETER … so you do not have to hack up your steak to check for doneness. It also takes the guess work out of cooking chicken and pork.

measure equivalents and metric conversions

1 cup = 8 ounces = 16 tablespoons = 237 milliliters

⅔ cup = 5 ounces = 11 tablespoons = 158 milliliters

½ cup = 4 ounces = 8 tablespoons = 118 milliliters

⅓ cup = 3 ounces = 5 tablespoons = 79 milliliters

¼ cup = 2 ounces = 4 tablespoons = 59 milliliters

1 tablespoon = 3 teaspoons = 15 milliliters

1 ounce = 28 grams

1 pound = 500 grams

1 cup = ¼ liter

1 pint = 20 ounces = 500 milliliters

1 quart = 40 ounces = 1 liter

what and how much do i need?

drinks

For most cocktail and dinner parties you can plan on about one alcohol drink per guest per hour, then round up the number.

A bottle of wine will give you four healthy size servings. Base your selection of red, white or rosé around the menu. A dry rosé is usually a nice compromise and will go with most foods. Dry rosé wines are very food friendly and often fly under the radar, and are perfect for almost any spring or summer event.

If you are serving spicy dishes, sparkling wine will work well. Sparkling wine is not only for toasts!

If the party is based around a sporting event then plan on more beer than wine. Plan on three beers per guy for every two hours.

You want at least two small bottles of water per guests.

If you are buying ice, plan on 1.5 pounds per guest. Add an extra bag if you are going to set up a cooler full of beer or soda.

eats

If you are hosting a two hour cocktail party, you will want 4-5 hors d'oeuvres per person per hour. Having a variety is crucial. Ideally you want 2-3 savory bites and 1-2 sweet ones.

If you are not planning a meal, at least two of the hors d'oeuvres should be substantial and based around a protein.

You will want to have food out from beginning to end. Assume that every guest will want to try at least one of everything you are serving. Guys eat more than women (no kidding), so if there will be mostly men then increase the food by 25%. If it is a Super Bowl party or related to a sporting event, increase the food by 50%.

Do not forget about vegetarians and guests with healthy eating habits. Have one or two substantial vegetarian hors d'oeuvres available.

Have several lemons and limes on hand when you are cooking for guests. Often a quick splash of fresh lemon or lime juice at the very end can wake up the flavors of the dish. Treat the citrus juice like you would salt and pepper in adjusting the seasoning before serving the dish.

Occasionally friends will bring friends without telling you and you find yourself having to feed more people than planned. Be prepared by always having your pantry stocked with high quality foods that make an instant antipasto platter. Jarred mushrooms, roasted peppers and olives along with crackers, (unsliced) salami and Marcona almonds can stay in your pantry for months without spoiling.

equipment

You are going to need serving platters and serving bowls. The first few times you entertain, you can buy nice disposable platters and bowls from a local party supply store. After a few parties that can get expensive, so it be would worthwhile to buy a few platters and bowls (either ceramic, glass or stainless steel). They do not have to match and you can buy them opportunistically on sale. It will make your life easier if everything you buy is dishwasher safe.

Think about what you are serving and make sure you have the right kind of serving utensils. You cannot serve soup with a big fork.

If you can find inexpensive stemless wine glasses, buy them. Intimate dinner parties are the time to break out the nice wine glasses. If you have over 10 guests, assume that at least one glass will break. The benefit of stemless glasses is that they will fit in the dishwasher. The last thing you want to see the morning after a party is a long row of glasses waiting to be cleaned.

You will go through more paper napkins than you think. Buy extra. Have both large dinner napkins and smaller cocktail napkins on hand.

top 10 assumptions for all of the recipes

1. ALWAYS read the recipe in its entirety before you start cooking.
2. Have salt and pepper nearby when cooking.
3. Salt should be kosher salt when cooking not table salt. The texture of the grains makes a difference.
4. Keep your knives sharp. Once a year take your knives to be professionally sharpened.
5. If a recipe calls for butter, use unsalted butter. Save the salted butter for spreading on toast.
6. When eggs are in a recipe use large eggs, not extra-large eggs.
7. Wash all fruits and vegetables before you use them---I don't care if they look clean.
8. Keep the cutting board clean and sanitary by wiping it down with white vinegar on a regular basis
9. Wash your hands, especially after working with onions or chili peppers.
10. Learn to trust your instincts and tastes when adjusting the salt and pepper in your dishes

culinary notes

2
SCOTCH TASTING AFFAIR

... Walnut chutney (to serve with duck proscitto)

... Duck prosciutto with walnut chutney

... Smoked trout rillettes

... Prime rib bites with mustard cream sauce

... Risotto Scotch eggs

... Dark chocolate tart with pretzel crust

Scotch Tasting Affair

"The proper drinking of Scotch whisky is more than indulgence; it is a toast to civilization."

David Daiches

Drinking Scotch the right way

FEW THINGS SPEAK OF A great night with the guys more than organizing a scotch tasting. Find a local liquor shop that has a friendly and knowledgeable staff to help select the whiskeys for your tasting. You do not want to use plastic or paper cups for the tasting since they can affect the flavor of the scotch. Often you can find inexpensive tumbler glasses at discount stores or warehouse clubs.

These recipes have enough flavor to stand up to the scotch but will not overpower or mask their nuances. You should also have plenty of water for your guests, both adding to the liquor as well as cleansing the palate between tastes.

You can have a very informal tasting or a structured event. If your guests will want to take notes, then it is fun to develop "cheat sheets" beforehand. Have sheets of paper with the name of each whisky written across the top of the page. At the side of each page, create categories for scribbling notes on the whisky's color, legs, bouquet, flavor, and finish. Provide pens for the guests.

some common terms used to describe the flavors in scotch whiskey

AUSTERE: Seemingly stern, severe, and unadorned in character.

BALANCED: One flavor or aroma element does not dominate.

BIG: Bold, dominant, hard to ignore flavors and presence in the mouth.

COMPLEX: Seeming to possess many layers of flavor.

DARK FLAVORS: Reminiscent of flavors like molasses.

FLORAL: can refer to both taste and aroma.

HARSH: An unpleasantly aggressive or caustic flavor or feeling to the mouth or nose.

MALT, MALTY: Refers to the aroma and flavor of malted barley.

MEDICINAL: Evocative of memories of liquid medicines.

NUTTY: Evocative of the taste of nuts, or reminiscent of the alkaloid qualities of some nuts.

OAKY: Influenced by aging in an oak cask. Implies a spicy, astringent character.

ORANGE, Orangey: Reminiscent of the fruit.

PEPPERY: Reminiscent of black pepper or hot chile peppers.

SHERRY: Influenced by aging in a sherry cask. Usually implies a sweet, somewhat winey character.

SMOKE, SMOKEY: Evocative of the flavor of smoke.

SPICY: Reminiscent of spices such as cinnamon, clove, or nutmeg.

SUBTLE: The elements of interest are not obvious on the palate.

SWEET: Either sweet in itself, or reminiscent of sweetness.

VEGETATIVE: Reminiscent of green plants.

YOUTHFUL: Full of vibrant, volatile, light characteristics. Think of a young wine.

WINEY: Reminiscent of wine.

WOODY: new wood, toasted old wood are variations of woody flavors.

walnut chutney
serve with duck prosciutto *(page 18)*

THE GREAT DEPTH OF FLAVOR and texture in this chutney will have you putting it on everything. In addition to serving with prosciutto, try it over poached salmon or grilled chicken.

Makes 2 cups

Core and finely chop the apple, jalapeño and shallot. Roughly chop the walnuts and dates.

Place the apple, shallots, jalapeño, nuts, raisins, sugar, cinnamon, ginger, zest, allspice, pepper flakes and hot sauce in a saucepan. Pour in the apple juice and vinegar. Bring to a boil.

Simmer gently, uncovered, until the chutney thickens to the consistency of molasses, about 30 - 45 minutes. Cool to room temperature and then store in a covered container in the refrigerator for up to 2 weeks.

SHOPPING LIST

- Golden Delicious apple, 1 medium
- Shallot, 1 medium
- Jalapeño, 1
- Chopped walnuts, ⅔ cup
- Golden raisins, ⅔ cup
- Dark brown sugar, ¾ cup firmly packed
- Ground cinnamon, 1 teaspoon
- Ground ginger, ½ teaspoon
- Orange zest, ½ teaspoon
- Ground allspice, ¼ teaspoon
- Red-pepper flakes, ¼ teaspoon
- Hot sauce, 3-4 splashes
- Apple Juice, ½ cup
- Apple cider vinegar, ½ cup

duck prosciutto with walnut chutney

THE PROSCIUTTO YOU FIND AT your local deli counter is a dry cured ham. It is delicious but very expensive. Making this version using duck is easy and you can amaze your guests with your charcuterie-making skills. One of the best parts of entertaining is regaling your guests with stories about how you prepared the food and this recipe will let you dazzle them. The walnut chutney is a nice accompaniment that will balance out the richness of the prosciutto. It has become easy to find duck breast in major supermarkets.

2 WEEKS AHEAD

In a bowl thoroughly mix together the sugar, salt, juniper berries, bay leaf crumbled up and 1 teaspoon of pepper.

Pour half of the salt mixture in the bottom of the glass dish.

Arrange duck breast halves, skin side up, in a single layer over salt. Top the duck with remaining salt mixture, pressing down to firmly plant the duck into the salt mixture. The duck should be completely covered by the mixture. Cover with plastic wrap and refrigerate 3 days. Remove duck from the salt mixture and wipe off all of the salt with paper towels. The duck breast will feel firmer and you will notice how much moisture was wicked out of the duck into the salt mixture.

Coat the duck breasts with the remaining teaspoon of pepper.

Place each breast half on a double layer of cheesecloth. Gather edges of cheesecloth together, tie together and hang duck in the back of your refrigerator for 2 weeks. There is usually some edge to the refrigerator shelves where you can hook the cheesecloth. You want to ensure that air is able to circulate all around the breast so it will cure evenly.

Overall the duck will lose about 30% of its weight during the curing process. It will become very firm and darker in color.

Makes 10 appetizer servings

TO SERVE

To serve, you will want to cut the breast as thin as you possibly can and serve on a white plate. Ideally the slices will be so thin they will be translucent. The color of the prosciutto is gorgeous and will leave your guests gushing over your culinary skills.

You can store it in an airtight container in refrigerator up to 5 days. Serve with crackers, baguette slices or apple slices.

Serve with walnut chutney *(see page 17)*.

SHOPPING LIST

Kosher salt, 4 cups

Sugar, 2 cups

Juniper berries, 10

Bay leaf

Fresh ground pepper, 2 teaspoons

Magret boneless duck breast halves, 2 (a total of 8 ounces)

EQUIPMENT

8x8 square glass baking dish

Mixing bowl

Plastic wrap

Cheese cloth

smoked trout rillettes

RILLETE IS A CLASSIC FRENCH dish similar to pâté, usually made with pork or duck. This is a slightly lighter version that is great around the holidays, but just as enjoyable during the summer when paired with a glass of sauvignon blanc. It is VERY easy to make and almost tastes better if made a day or two in advance so the flavors can meld. It has become common to find smoked trout at large supermarkets, often at the deli counters.

Let the butter come to room temperature.

Remove the skin and bones from the smoked trout. There are a lot of small bones in the trout, take the time to carefully remove all of them. You do not want guests to be surprised by finding small bones. Break the trout meat up into chunky pieces about the size of your fingernail.

Chop the green onion into fine pieces. Mince ½ the shallot into very fine pieces.

Juice the lemon; you want to have about 1½ tablespoons of lemon juice.

In a mixing bowl, thoroughly blend the butter, mascarpone cheese, shallots, green onion and most but not all of the lemon juice so it becomes a smooth consistency. Add the trout to the mixture and carefully mix together.

Season to taste with salt, pepper, and the remaining lemon juice, if desired. The smoked trout already brings saltiness to this dish, so go light on any additional salt. You want to be able to still see small chunks of trout in the otherwise smooth mixture.

If you make this in advance, let it stand at room temperature one hour before serving.

Makes 6-8 Servings

TO ASSEMBLE

You can make this dish up to 2 days before the party and store it in the refrigerator.

Serve the rillettes surrounded with crackers or baguette slices. Provide a small knife or spoon so guest can spread the rillettes on the crackers or bread.

SHOPPING LIST

Smoked trout, about 7 ounces which will produce 1 ½ cups when the skin and bones are removed. (Can substitute hot smoked salmon if you cannot find trout.)

Mascarpone cheese, 4 ounces

Butter, 3 tablespoons (room temperature)

Green onion, about 2 stalks

Shallot, 1 medium size

Lemon, 1 large

Splash of hot sauce

Assorted crackers or a sliced baguette

EQUIPMENT

mixing bowl

Scotch Tasting Affair

prime rib bites with mustard cream sauce

THIS HORS D'OEUVRE IS FULL of meaty goodness. You want to marinate the meat for at least 6 hours, but letting it sit in the marinade overnight is even better.

DO THE DAY BEFORE

Trim away the big pieces of fat and cut the rib-eye into 1 inch cubes. Place in a gallon size self-sealing disposable plastic bag along with the vegetable oil. Roughly chop the garlic and rosemary and add to the bag along with a pinch of salt and pepper. Place the bag in the refrigerator for the meat to marinate several hours or overnight and shake up the bag every few hours. It helps to place the bag on a plate in case any marinade leaks out of the bag.

Make the mustard cream sauce up to a day ahead and store covered in the refrigerator. Whisk together the sour cream, mustard, honey, and 1 teaspoon of lemon zest in small bowl. Season to taste with salt and pepper.

Makes enough appetizers to serve 8

WHEN READY TO SERVE

Remove the marinated meat from the refrigerator 30 minutes before you plan on cooking. Heat the pan over medium high heat. Place the first batch of steak cubes into the hot pan, do not overcrowd. The pieces should not be touching each other. As the meat gets brown on one side, turn and brown on another side. Keep turning until the meat is browned on all sides. By the time all the sides are browned, the middle of the steak cubes should be medium (pink and warm). Depending on the size of your pan, you will have to do this in 3-4 batches.

As the cubes are done, set aside on a plate which allows the meat to rest. When all of the cubes are cooked, place on a platter with a bowl of the mustard dipping cream sauce in the middle. Place toothpicks in the individual steak cubes for easy access by your guests.

SHOPPING LIST

Rib-eye steaks, 2 thick steaks, about 1 inch thick

Garlic, 2 cloves

Rosemary, 3-4 branches

Vegetable oil, 1 cup

Sour cream, 1 cup

Dijon mustard, 1 cup

Honey, 1 teaspoon

Lemon, 1 small for zest

EQUIPMENT

Small mixing bowl

Large saute pan or cast iron skillet

Toothpicks for serving

risotto scotch eggs

MY INSPIRATION FOR THIS DISH is a combination of scotch eggs and risotto balls. Scotch eggs are usually found in English style pubs. It is a hardboiled egg wrapped in sausage, breaded and deep fried. They are satisfying and filling, but are basically a heart-attack on a plate. Risotto balls are commonplace in wine bars and are delicious at room temperature. This recipe takes the best of both of these classic dishes and combines them with a lighter more contemporary twist. You can make this recipe a day in advance and just reheat to serve.

Finely chop the onion and garlic.

Melt 2 tablespoons of butter in a large saucepan over medium heat and add chopped onion and garlic. Sauté until onions are translucent, about 5 minutes, be careful that the garlic does not burn. Remove casing from the sausage and sauté until fully cooked and brown. While cooking the sausage, break it up with a spoon. The sausage pieces should be no bigger than twice the size of a grain of rice. Add rice; stir 1 minute so the rice can absorb some of the butter and fat released from the sausage (fat = flavor). Add the wine and reduce heat to medium-low. Simmer until wine is mostly absorbed and there is almost no liquid left in the pan. Add about 2 cups of broth to the pan. Stir until broth is almost absorbed, around 5 minutes. Add 3 more cups of broth 1 cup at a time, allowing broth to be mostly absorbed before adding the next cup. Cook until rice is tender and mixture is creamy, 25 minutes total. If the rice is not tender enough, add the remaining cup of broth. Mix in cheese, remaining 3 tablespoons butter and season with salt and pepper. Let cool completely.

Preheat oven to 400° F.

Makes 16 servings

EASIEST WAY TO BOIL EGGS

Place 8 eggs in a saucepan and add enough cold tap water to cover completely the eggs by 1 inch. Bring to a rolling boil over high heat. Once the water is boiling, turn off the heat and leave covered for 10 minutes. After 10 minutes place eggs under ice cold water or in a bowl of ice and water to chill. Leave them for a few minutes in the cold water until the egg is completely cooled. This step keeps the yolk bright yellow and prevents a greenish "ring" from forming on the surface of the yolk. Peel the shell from the eggs and set the eggs aside.

ASSEMBLY

Cut the shelled and cooked eggs into quarters and fill the shallow bowl with bread crumbs. Use the chilled risotto to wrap a layer around each egg quarter to completely encase the egg. The risotto should be sticky enough that it will adhere to the egg. After covering the egg, gently roll in bread crumbs to coat with a thin layer. They will be delicate so be gentle with them.

Place the coated eggs on a baking sheet lined with a silicone pad or parchment paper, spray them with vegetable spray and bake for 20 minutes or until they are golden brown. Let them cool for 10 minutes before serving. They are also delicious served at room temperature.

SHOPPING LIST

Eggs, 8

Mild Italian sausage, 8 ounces

Panko bread crumbs, 16 ounces

Butter, 5 tablespoons

Small onion, 1

Garlic clove, 1

Arborio rice, 1 pound

Dry white wine, 1 cup

Low-salt chicken broth, 6 cups

Grated Parmesan cheese, 6 cups

Vegetable oil spray

EQUIPMENT

Sauce pan with a lid

A shallow bowl

Baking sheet

Silicone non-stick pad or parchment paper

dark chocolate tart with pretzel crust

THIS RECIPE WAS INSPIRED BY my love of chocolate covered pretzels. The saltiness and crunch of the pretzels plays off the deep richness of the chocolate. Using a fluted tart pan really helps in the presentation and is worth the tiny investment to buy one. The tart pan can also be used to make quiche – and real gentlemen do eat quiche. Because this is such a rich and decadent dessert you want to serve your guests thin slices. Make this dessert at least 6 hours or up to a day before you want to serve it.

To make the crust, use an electric mixer. Beat the butter with ¾ of a cup of crushed pretzels and the confectioners' sugar at low speed until the mixture becomes creamy and lighter in color. Slowly add the flour and egg. Add another ½ cup of pretzels, being sure to leave some larger pretzel pieces in the dough to provide crunch. The dough will have the consistency of clay (don't worry, it does not taste like clay!). Flatten the dough between two sheets of plastic wrap and press down until the disc becomes the size of a Frisbee, 11-12 inches in diameter. Refrigerate until chilled, at least one hour but could be up to four hours.

Preheat the oven to 350° F.

Peel off the top sheet of plastic wrap and invert the dough over a 10-inch fluted tart pan with a removable bottom. Use your hands to carefully press the dough into the pan so it covers the bottom in an even layer and comes up all the way on the sides. The dough is forgiving and you can use your fingers to patch any tears. Put the dough back into the refrigerator for 30 minutes or until firm.

Makes 16-20 servings

Line the dough shell with parchment paper and fill with the beans. The parchment paper is important to use so the dried beans do not accidently become part of your dessert. Bake for about 30 minutes, the dough should be firm and nearly set. Remove the parchment and beans and bake for another 10 to 15 minutes, until the tart shell is firm and slightly darker brown in color. You can keep the beans for the next time you will bake pie crusts or just throw out. Let the tart cool completely.

While the tart shell is baking, make the filling. In a saucepan, bring the cream to a slow boil. Add the chocolate, pinch of salt and then take off the heat. Whisk with a spoon until all of the chocolate is melted and the mixture is smooth. If the chocolate is not fully melted, return the saucepan to medium heat for a minute or two. Let the chocolate mixture cool for 5 minutes.

Pour the filling into the shell, and spread around until the chocolate is an even layer. Sprinkle with remaining pretzels in a decorative pattern and refrigerate until the chocolate is firm, at least 6 hours or overnight.

SHOPPING LIST

Unsalted butter 4 ounces (one stick)

Thin pretzels, 4 ounces or about 1 ¾ cups

Confectioners' sugar ¾ cup

All-purpose flour ½ cup

Egg, 1

Heavy cream 1 ½ cups

Bittersweet chocolate, 12 ounces, morsel or chopped. If you have options, pick a dark chocolate in the 60-70% cocoa range.

Any dried beans, 2 cups (they are not for eating and you will throw them out after using them)

EQUIPMENT

Stand mixer

10-inch fluted tart pan with a removable bottom

Medium saucepan

Parchment paper

culinary notes

culinary notes

3
SUPER BOWL/MARCH MADNESS

- Tomatillo guacamole salsa with homemade chips
- Edamame dip
- Pork, pork, pork and sauerkraut stew
- Bison lollipops in dried cherry sauce
- Turkey sliders with chipotle thousand island dressing
- Italian Macaroni Pie
- "Jambalaya" bread pudding
- Sweet potato salad with mustard greens and bacon vinaigrette
- Sinful vanilla bourbon rice pudding

REMEMBER THAT WHEN YOU HAVE friends over to watch a big game that it is all about the game. The food and drinks should not be a distraction. Dishes, like these recipes, should be easy to eat and able to stay out for a while and be easy to prepare and serve. You do not want to miss the game by being stuck in the kitchen.

Set up two coolers with ice, one filled with beer and one filled with soda and bottled water near the television. You should have an equal number of alcoholic and non-alcoholic drinks. Remember, your friends still have to drive home.

Put the beers on ice at least two hours before the game starts. Having your friends arrive to warm beer is justification for them to slap you around.

Don't put out all of your food at the same time. Put out several smaller dishes and hors d'oeuvres at the beginning of the game, heartier dishes before halftime and coffee along with desserts at the beginning of the fourth quarter. By staggering the food, it will keep things interesting for your guests.

Unless you are still in college, forget about drinking games!

It is fine to use disposable everything; paper plates, plastic utensils, plastic cups, etc. You will have a better time if you do not have to worry about washing dishes later. There are also environmentally friendlier options such as bamboo plates and utensils made with recycled plastic.

After several hours of eating and drinking, guests will not be expecting elaborate desserts. High quality store bought cookies and brownies will work great.

If guys are going to bring girlfriends, wives or kids then have a separate room with other options for them so they can still have an enjoyable evening AND do not distract the guests who are seriously into the game.

Betting pools are a way to keep everyone engaged in the game. Keep the stakes low so that all of your guests will feel comfortable participating and no one will have trouble making their next mortgage payment if they lose.

Super Bowl/March Madness

tomatillo guacamole salsa

THIS RECIPE BLENDS THE BEST of two classic dips: salsa and guacamole. It packs a ton of flavor with a nice kick of heat from the peppers.

SHOPPING LIST

Tomatillos, 1 pound

Cilantro, 1 bunch

Garlic, 2 cloves

Ripe avocados, 3

Serrano peppers, 4

Limes, 3 for juice

Tortilla chips or corn tortillas

EQUIPMENT

Food processor

Mixing bowl

Makes about 2 cups, enough for 8-10 people

Remove the outer husks from the tomatillos and rinse. Roast tomatillos, Serrano peppers and garlic under broiler until they are tender. Be careful that the garlic does not burn. When the vegetables are done, transfer them to the food processor, and let them cool for 10 minutes.

Purée the tomatillos, garlic and peppers, transfer the mixture to a mixing bowl and salt to taste (don't be shy with the salt). Remove the leaves from around 7-8 cilantro stems and chop the leaves, add to the mixture. Cut the avocados in half lengthwise. Carefully remove the large pit and use a spoon to scoop out the flesh. If the avocado is ripe, this is easy work. Chop the flesh into small pieces and stir it into the tomatillo mixture. Juice the limes and add the juice to the mixture and blend thoroughly. You can make this a day ahead and refrigerate, just do not add the avocado until you are ready to serve.

TO SERVE

Serve the salsa with tortilla chips. You can also make your own chips. Cut corn tortillas into 6 pieces. Pour 1 inch of oil in a large skillet and heat to 350° F. You will know if the oil is hot enough if you drop a tortilla piece into it and the tortilla immediately begins to sizzle. Fry for 3-4 minutes until they are crisp and salt as soon as you remove them from the oil. Let them drain on a paper towel lined plate.

edamame dip

THIS IS A HEALTHY DIP that is so delicious it does not taste healthy! Serve it with tortilla chips or pita bread. Edamame is a Japanese product that is increasingly easy to find in the freezer section of supermarkets. It is low in fat and high in protein. This is a satisfying treat if you have athletic guys over who want to eat healthy.

Makes 8-10 servings

You might have to remove the edamame from their pods and discard the pods. Roughly chop ¼ of the onion and 5-6 pieces of cilantro. Place the edamame, onion, cilantro, garlic, lemon juice, miso, chili paste and honey into the bowl of a food processor and process for 15 seconds. Stop to scrape down the sides of the bowl and process for another 15 to 20 seconds. Salt and pepper to taste.

With the processor running, slowly drizzle in the olive oil. Once all of the oil has been added, stop, scrape down the bowl and then process another 5 to 10 seconds. Taste and adjust salt and pepper as needed. Store in an airtight container for up to 5 days.

SHOPPING LIST

Edamame, 12 ounces pre-cooked

Onion, 1 small

Cilantro, ½ bunch

Garlic, 1 large clove

Lemons, 2 for juice

Brown miso, 1 tablespoon* (optional)

Red chili paste, 1 tablespoon (or to taste)

Olive oil, 5 tablespoons

Honey ½ tablespoon

Tortilla chips or pita bread

EQUIPMENT

Food processor

*You might have to go to an Asian market to find brown miso. I think the miso adds a lot of flavor to the dish, but the dip is still amazing even if you skip the miso.

pork, pork, pork and sauerkraut stew

THREE DIFFERENT KINDS OF PORK provide depth of flavor and texture to the stew. This dish is always a big hit and can stay out the entire game if you have a crock pot. It is a very satisfying dish that goes great with beer.

Place the dried mushroom and 1 1/2 cups of hot water into a bowl. Let the mushrooms reconstitute for 1 hour. Drain and reserve water.

Heat oven to 350° F.

Cut the bacon into 1 inch pieces and cook it in a large pot over medium heat until crisp, 6-8 minutes. Using a slotted spoon, remove and set aside leaving the bacon fat in the pot.

Remove the bone from the smoked pork chops and cut into ½ inch pieces. Cut the kielbasa into ½ inch pieces. Add pork chops and kielbasa to the pot and increase heat to medium-high; cook until browned, 10-12 minutes.

Makes 8-10 servings

Thinly slice the onions. Using a slotted spoon, remove the meat and set aside. Add allspice, dry mustard, bay leaves and onions. Cook for 8-10 minutes, until the onions become soft. Make sure to scrape up browned bits on the bottom of the pot; that is pure flavor. Add tomato paste and cook for 5-6 minutes until the tomato paste turns from bright red to dark almost rust color. Dice the mushrooms and along with sauerkraut add to the pot. Cook for 12–14 minutes. Add mushroom water, all the meat, wine, stock and bring to a boil. Season with salt and pepper to taste; cover pot with foil or a lid. Braise in oven until meat is cooked through and tender, about 30 minutes.

If you have a crock pot, skip the oven and let it cook for 1 hour on high and place the crock pot directly out for your guests to enjoy. It will stay warm the entire game on the low setting.

SHOPPING LIST

Dried porcini mushrooms, ¼ ounce

Thick cut bacon, ½ pound

Smoked pork chops, 1 pound

Smoked kielbasa, ½ pound

Allspice, 2 teaspoons

Dry mustard, 1 teaspoon

Bay leaves, 2

Yellow onions, 2 large

Tomato paste, 4.5 ounces (one tube)

Sauerkraut, 4 pounds

White wine, 2 cups
(use a fruity white wine with no oak)

Low Sodium chicken stock, 1 cup

EQUIPMENT

A large crock pot helps but not necessary

Large pot

bison lollipops in dried cherry sauce

BISON (BUFFALO) MEAT HAS BECOME widely popular because it is lower in fat than ground beef. I love it because it has great flavor and this recipe will have your guests grazing all game. You can make this dish up to two days in advance.

MEATBALLS

Finely mince the shallot and garlic. In a large bowl mix ground bison with salt, pepper, shallot, egg, garlic chili paste, thyme and combine thoroughly with your hands. Shape mixture into 1 inch meatballs. Wash your hands.

Heat oil in a large skillet over medium-high heat until hot. Add meatballs in batches, and cook until browned, turning often. Remove meatballs from skillet with a slotted spoon and set aside.

Makes 8-10 servings

SAUCE

Roughly chop the onion. Over medium heat cook chopped onion in pan drippings until they turn golden in color. Stir in tomato paste and cook until paste begins to brown. Stir in cherries, bay leaf, thyme sprigs, wine, vinegar and broth. Cook over medium-high heat, scraping the bits of flavor that cling to bottom of skillet. Bring mixture to a boil, and cook until liquid is reduced by about ⅔ and the sauce begins to thicken. Salt and pepper to taste and discard bay leaf and thyme sprigs.

Using an immersion blender or traditional blender, blend the sauce until very smooth. Add meatballs to sauce in the skillet pan and heat for 5 minutes. You can make the meatballs and sauce up to 2 days in advance. Store separately in the refrigerator. To reheat, add meatballs to cherry sauce and cook until the meatballs are heated through. Transfer meatballs and sauce to a large platter and insert toothpicks into each meatball.

SHOPPING LIST

Bison, 2 pounds ground

Salt, 2 teaspoons

Ground pepper, 2 teaspoons

Shallot, 1

Garlic, 2 cloves

Garlic chili paste, 3 tablespoons

Dried thyme, 1 teaspoon

Egg, 1 large

Vegetable oil, 3 tablespoons

Onion, 1 small

Tomato paste, 2 tablespoons

Dried cherries, 9 ounces

Bay leaf, 1

Fresh thyme, 2 sprigs

Red wine, 1 cup
   Merlot or Malbec work great

Balsamic vinegar, 3 tablespoons

Low sodium chicken broth, 22 ounces

EQUIPMENT

Blender or immersion mixer

Large skillet

Toothpicks

Super Bowl/March Madness

turkey sliders with chipotle thousand island dressing

DO NOT BE FOOLED BY the turkey in this recipe. Its purpose is not to be healthier than ground beef … it is all about the taste! The Chipotle Thousand Island dressing puts these little guys over the top.

TURKEY

You can mix up the turkey meat with spices a day in advance and cook when ready to serve.

Finely mince the shallot. In a mixing bowl add shallots, turkey, chili paste, parmesan cheese and season with salt and pepper. Use your hands to combine everything gently but thoroughly.

Divide the turkey mixture into 8 portions and form into patties. When making the patties, consider the size of the rolls you have. They should match. It is easy to find small rolls, or dinner rolls that are around 2 to 3 inches in diameter. A slider should be able to be consumed in 2-3 bites (or one really large bite if your friends are like mine).

Heat a large skillet with the vegetable oil over moderately high heat until hot. Cook the patties, turning over once, until just cooked through (no longer pink), 4 to 5 minutes for each side.

TO SERVE

Toast the rolls and slather on the Thousand Island dressing, place the patty on the bun and top with a slice of cheese.

Makes 8 sliders

CHIPOTLE THOUSAND ISLAND DRESSING

You can make the Thousand Island dressing up to a week in advance; just make sure you do not use all of it before your party. It is so tasty, that you will be tempted to slather it on everything. Finely chop 2 chipotle peppers. Add to a mixing bowl along with 1 tablespoon of the adobo tomato sauce packed with the peppers. Add in mayonnaise, ketchup, juice from 1 lemon, pickle relish and mustard. Mix to combine and store in the refrigerator.

Why choose turkey?

.... Because the union of turkey and chipotle Thousand Island sauce works like a swiss back rub; just the right touch

SHOPPING LIST

Ground turkey, 1 ½ pounds (dark meat or a combination of white and dark meat)

Shallot, 1 large

Vegetable oil, 2 tablespoons

Garlic chili paste, 2 tablespoons

Parmesan cheese, 2 ounces

Vegetable oil, 1 tablespoon

Extra-sharp Cheddar, 8 slices, (5 ounces)

Small rolls, 8

Low-fat mayonnaise, 1 cup

Ketchup, 2 tablespoons

Lemon, 1 for juice

Sweet pickle relish, 1 tablespoon

Dijon mustard, 2 tablespoons

Chipotle peppers in adobo sauce, small can

EQUIPMENT

Large skillet pan

Mixing bowl

italian macaroni pie

I THINK OF THIS AS the most amazing baked ziti EVER! It can be prepared in advance and the ingredients are not very expensive. It would also taste great the next day, but every time I make it there are never any leftovers.

Cut the porchetta (or ham) into ½ inch cubes. Grate the carrot and onion. If you do not have a grater, then finely mince the vegetables.

Heat the pot over high heat and add the vegetable oil. Cook the porchetta for 10 minutes. It will start to brown. Add the carrot, onion and spinach and cook until the vegetables are very tender, about 10 minutes. Add the wine, bring to a boil and cook until the wine is reduced by half, about 5 minutes. Add the tomato sauce and reduce the heat to low, cover the pan, and cook until the meat is very tender, about 2 hours. Ham is leaner with less connective tissue, so if you substitute, it will take about an hour. Keep the sauce warm.

Preheat the oven to 375° F.

Bring 6 quarts of water to a boil in a large pot and add 2 tablespoons salt.

Cook the ziti in the boiling water for 1 minute less than the package directions say, the ziti will be very *al dente*. The pasta will continue cooking in the sauce. While the pasta is cooking, place the ricotta in a small bowl and stir in a ladle of the boiling water from the pasta. That will melt the ricotta cheese creating a smooth and creamy mixture.

Drain the pasta using a strainer and add it to the sauce. Cut the provolone into small pieces. Add the melted ricotta, provolone and basil and stir to combine.

Fill a 9 x 13-inch baking dish with the pasta, cheese and meat mixture. Sprinkle the parmigiano-reggiano cheese over the top and bake for 30 minutes until bubbly and the cheese has browned.

Makes 8-10 hearty portions

SHOPPING LIST

Vegetable oil, 2 tablespoons

Butter, 1 tablespoon

Porchetta*, 1 ¼ pound
(can substitute ham)

Carrot, 1 small

Onion, 1

Red wine, 1 ½ cups

Dry basil, 1 tablespoon

Jar of quality tomato sauce, 24 ounces

Ziti, 1 ½ pounds

Fresh ricotta, 1 pound

Frozen chopped spinach, 1 pound

Provolone cheese, 8 ounces

Parmigiano-reggiano, ½ cup grated

EQUIPMENT

Large pot with a lid

Box grater

Large pot (to cook the pasta)

Strainer

9 x 13 inch baking dish

Porchetta is an Italian pork roast that has layers of stuffing and tons of flavor. It is increasingly easy to find at the deli counters in major supermarkets or in Italian delis.

The other pie

NOT PIZZA!

A gentleman knows the value in preparing quality meals for guests, he also knows that ordering pizza is like giving up on the night.

....
....
....

Knife & FORK Required

"jambalaya" bread pudding

THIS RECIPE INCORPORATES THE SAME key ingredients as the classic version. Instead of rice, this recipe embeds the flavors in a savory bread pudding. It results in a lighter dish that packs the same huge flavor punch as the classic. This dish is great for entertaining since you can prep it in earlier in the day and then just put it in the oven to bake an hour before you want to serve.

DO A FEW HOURS AHEAD

Cut the fully cooked sausage in half lengthwise then thinly sliced crosswise. The result will be thin, half-moon shaped slices. Set aside in the refrigerator.

Cook the shrimp. If they are not already out of their shells, peel them. In a sauce pan, poach the shrimp in wine (or beer), lemon cut in half and 2 cups of water and tablespoon of salt. Add more water if there is not enough liquid to completely cover the shrimp. The shrimp should cook over a medium low heat until they are just barely cooked through. They will finish cooking in the pudding. Set aside.

Cut the cooked chicken into small cubes (about ¾ inch cubes). Set aside.

(continued on page 44)

Makes 8-10 servings

SHOPPING LIST

High quality white bread or an "eggy" bread such as brioche or Challah, 2 unsliced loaves

Andouille sausages or other fully cooked smoked spicy sausages (such as Louisiana hot links), 1 pound

Medium size shrimp (31/40), ¾ of a pound. It is easier if they are purchased peeled and de-veined.

Chicken meat, ½ pound. The dark meat from roasted chicken you find in supermarkets works well. If you can find Tasso, the spicy ham, that would be a great substitution for the chicken!

Lemon, 1

Eggs, 5

White wine (anything but Chardonnay) or pilsner-style ale, 4 ounces

Whole milk, 1 cup

Heavy cream, 3 cups

Butter, 5 tablespoons

Yellow onion, 1 medium yellow chopped

Red bell pepper, 1 chopped into small pieces

Green onions, 5 stalks with just the green part thinly sliced

Celery, 1 stalk sliced

Garlic, 5 cloves finely chopped

Dried cayenne pepper, 2 teaspoons

Dried thyme, 1 teaspoon (or 2 teaspoons fresh thyme)

Hot sauce (optional)

Worcestershire sauce, 1 teaspoon

Can of diced tomatoes (14 ½ ounce), drained of the juice

Parmesan cheese, 4 ounces grated

EQUIPMENT

9 x 13 inch baking dish

Sauté pan, 10 or 12 inch

Vegetable spray

Very large mixing bowl

"jambalaya" bread pudding *(continued)*

WHEN READY TO ASSEMBLE

Preheat the oven to 350° F.

Take 1 ½ loaves of bread and cut the crust off the bread, then cut the bread into 1 inch cubes. You should end up with about 12 cups bread cubes. Set aside so the bread will dry out slightly while preparing the other steps.

Heat 3 tablespoons of butter in the sauté pan over medium heat. Add sausages; sauté until lightly brown, about 5 minutes. Using slotted spoon, transfer sausages to a plate lined with paper towels but keep the drippings in the pan.

To the same pan with the retained drippings, add the 2 remaining tablespoons of butter. Sauté the onion, green onion, pepper and celery over medium heat. Sprinkle the cayenne powder, thyme, salt and pepper over the vegetables while they are sautéing. If you want to increase the spice level, add a few splashes of hot sauce. When the vegetables are cooked through but not mushy, about 10 minutes, set aside to let cool.

Coat the 9 x 13 inch pan with a vegetable spray so the pudding does not stick.

In the biggest bowl you have, lightly whisk the eggs, milk, cream, a generous pinch of salt, pinch of pepper, splash of hot sauce and Worcestershire sauce. Add the drained tomatoes, sausage, chicken, shrimp and sautéed vegetables. Add the bread cubes and stir well so the bread is thoroughly coated in the liquid. Let it sit for 15 minutes so the bread soaks up everything.

Add the mixture to the baking pan. Push the mixture down so that it is fully submerged in the liquid. Add the parmesan cheese in an even layer on top.

If you do not have a bowl big enough to fit everything, add the bread, meats, and vegetables to the baking dish and then beat the eggs, milk, cream, and Worcestershire sauce separately. Pour in the baking dish, making sure it is evenly distributed and all of the bread is completely soaked in the egg/milk liquid.

Sprinkle the parmesan cheese in an even layer over the top.

Bake for 40-45 minutes or until the pudding is moderately firm and the top is brown and bubbling. Let cool for 10 minutes before serving.

sweet potato salad with mustard greens and bacon vinaigrette

THIS IS ONE OF MY favorite side dishes. It is spicy, sweet, earthy and "bacony." It looks great on a buffet table with the rich color of the sweet potatoes and the vibrant color of the greens. Preheat oven to 300°F.

Makes 8-10 servings

Cook the bacon in large skillet until crisp. Transfer to a plate lined with paper towels to drain the bacon. When cool enough to handle, crumble bacon into large pieces and set aside. Keep around 2 tablespoons of the rendered bacon fat.

Dice the sweet potatoes into ½ inch cubes. Spray the baking sheet with the vegetable spray, lay the potatoes out in a single layer and sprinkle with salt. Bake the sweet potatoes until tender, about 25 minutes.

Cut the mustard greens into pieces ½ inch long and set aside.

Whisk together red wine vinegar, Dijon mustard, honey, juice from 1 lemon, hot sauce and reserved bacon fat in a small bowl. Whisk in olive oil and season with salt and pepper to taste.

When the potatoes come out of the oven, place in a large mixing bowl. Add 2 tablespoons of dressing to the potatoes, and the potatoes will soak up the dressing. Add the bacon and mustard greens. The heat of the potatoes will wilt the greens just enough. Add enough additional dressing to coat everything without starting to pool at the bottom of the bowl. Season with salt and pepper if needed. You can make this dish a few hours ahead; just cover and let stand at room temperature.

SHOPPING LIST

Red wine vinegar, 3 tablespoons

Dijon mustard, 3 tablespoons

Honey, 1 ½ tablespoons

Hot sauce, 7-8 splashes (1 ½ teaspoons hot pepper sauce)

Lemon, 1 for juice

Olive oil, 7 tablespoons

Sweet potatoes, 2 pounds

Bacon, 6 slices

Mustard greens, 10 large leaves (you can substitute kale, Swiss chard or turnip greens)

EQUIPMENT

Large skillet

Baking sheet

Vegetable spray

sinful vanilla bourbon rice pudding

GROWING UP, RICE PUDDING WAS always one of my favorite desserts. Only as an adult did I learn how much better it is once you add alcohol. You can make this dessert up to two days in advance.

In a small bowl combine bourbon and raisins and set aside for at least 1 hour so the raisins can plump up.

Combine milk, sugar, cinnamon stick and rice in the saucepan. Bring to a gentle simmer over medium heat, then reduce heat and cook uncovered for 1 hour, stirring occasionally. The milk should just barely simmer, with bubbles breaking only at the outside edge of the surface. After an hour, the rice should be very soft.

Drain the raisins (the bourbon makes a flavorful shot for the cook) and add to the rice. Remove the cinnamon stick. Increase the heat to medium, and cook, stirring frequently now, until the rice has absorbed most of the rest of the milk – but not all -- and the pudding is creamy, about 20 minutes longer. You have to keep stirring to ensure that it does not burn.

Remove from the heat and stir in the vanilla. Cool thoroughly then chill in the refrigerator. As it chills, the pudding will thicken. After a few hours in the refrigerator it will be quite thick, and probably no longer loose enough to be called "creamy." Before serving, stir in as much as ½ cup of cream to get the consistency you like. Serve chilled.

Makes 8-10 servings

SHOPPING LIST

Whole milk, 1 ½ quarts

Sugar, ⅔ cup

Long grain rice, ½ cup

Raisins, ½ cup

Cinnamon, 1 stick

Vanilla extract, 2 teaspoons

Bourbon, ½ cup

Heavy cream, ½ cup

EQUIPMENT

Saucepan

Every day is a sunny day

...When Eating Sinful Pudding

Simply add

Super Bowl/March Madness

culinary notes

culinary notes

Super Bowl/March Madness

4 CHEESE AND WINE PARTY

- Paprika candied pecans
- Garlic and thyme marinated warmed olives
- Dates stuffed with blue cheese mousse
- Parmesan crisps with goat cheese and chive mousse
- Savory jam elephant ears (palmiers)
- Tarragon chicken skewers with pistachio cream sauce
- Balsamic chocolate truffles

ORGANIZING A CHEESE AND WINE party is all about having fun with zero pretentiousness! It is worth the effort in finding a local liquor store or wine shop that has a friendly and knowledgeable staff. They can help you pick an interesting variety of wines to serve. It is easier if you give them a theme to work with, such as Italian red wines under $25/bottle, sparkling wines from California, etc. This is not the time to play it safe; try wines from regions you never had before or varietals that you cannot pronounce.

For tasting, one bottle will serve 9-10 guests – plan for two ounce (75-80ml) servings. You usually do not want to have your guests taste more than 6 different wines; otherwise they might become overnight guests. Always have plenty of water for guests to drink between wine tastings.

Three to four different well-selected cheeses are all you will need. Mix it up, pair together hard cheese, semi-soft cheese and soft cheese. Take your cheeses out of the refrigerator at least one hour before serving them. When cheeses are very cold, it masks their full flavor and aroma.

a few suggested wine-cheese pairings to use as a starting point

Cabernet Sauvignon — aged Cheddar, Blue or Colby
Champagne — Camembert or Gruyere
Chardonnay — Spanish goat cheese, Munster or Gruyere
Chateauneuf-Du-Pape — hard sheep's milk or aged Gouda
Chianti — Mozzarella, fontina or provolone
Gewurztraminer — Taleggio or other soft/semi-soft stinky cheeses
Malbec — mild blue cheese or manchego
Merlot — sheep's milk cheese or parmesan
Pinot Noir — Mild cheddar or mild Brie
Sauvignon Blanc — Cheshire or Spanish goat cheese
Viognier — Camembert
Zinfandel — aggressive blue cheese or Emmentaler

paprika candied pecans

THESE SPICY SWEET NUTS ARE addictive and go perfectly with almost any beer or wine. They will last a few days in an air-tight container, but it is hard to imagine they will not be consumed almost immediately. I also find these pecans to be just the thing when I am sitting on the couch with a special friend in my arms watching television.

Makes about 2 cups, enough for 6-8 guests at a party or 2 people watching a long movie

Preheat oven to 325° F.

Place the pecans on the baking sheet and place in the oven for 10 minutes. The pecans will be warm, but will not start to darken yet. Remove from oven and set aside.

Combine maple syrup, honey, salt, pepper, cinnamom, cayenne and paprika in large bowl. Stir to blend. Add the warm pecans and stir gently to evenly coat the nuts. Line the baking sheet with the silicone pad or parchment paper. Spread nuts onto the baking sheet in a single layer.

Bake until pecans are dark golden brown and the glaze is bubbling, about 10-12 minutes. You have to watch the nuts carefully because the honey and maple syrup can burn easily.

Let the pecans cool and break apart any pecans that are sticking to each other.

SHOPPING LIST

Maple syrup, 1 ½ tablespoons

Honey, 1 ½ tablespoons

Salt, ¾ teaspoon

Freshly ground black pepper, ¼ teaspoon

Cayenne pepper, 1 teaspoon

Cinnamon, ½ teaspoon

Smoked paprika, 1 teaspoon

Raw pecan pieces, 2 cups

EQUIPMENT

Baking sheet

Non-stick silicone pad or parchment paper

Mixing bowl

garlic and thyme marinated warmed olives

SERVING THESE OLIVES WARM BRINGS out their aromatic qualities and lusciousness. It is increasingly common to find quality olives sold in bulk at large supermarkets. Start with quality olives and this recipe takes them over the top. There is something very sexy about these olives that women cannot get enough of. There have been studies that have shown garlic and olives to be aphrodisiacs.

SHOPPING LISTS

Olives, 1 pound of a variety such as Kalamata or Picholine (about 3 cups)

Garlic, 2 heads or 12 cloves

Thyme, 8 large sprigs

Small lemon, 1 for zest

Extra-virgin olive oil, 3 cups

Bay leaf, 1

EQUIPMENT

Sauce pan

Toothpicks for serving

Makes about 3 ½ cups, enough for 6-8 guests

Separate the garlic heads into individual cloves and peel the cloves. Slice the garlic into thick pieces.

In a large saucepan, combine the olives with the garlic, thyme, bay leaf lemon zest and olive oil and bring to a simmer over low heat. Cook over low heat until the garlic is tender, about 20-25 minutes. You do not want the oil to boil otherwise the garlic will burn before it can become tender. Discard the herb sprigs and bay leaf. Using a slotted spoon, transfer the olives and garlic to a bowl. Let cool slightly and serve warm with toothpicks.

The olives can be prepared up to 3 days ahead and refrigerated in the oil; warm gently before serving.

dates stuffed with blue cheese mousse

THIS DISH IS SO EASY to make and is the perfect finger food to pair with sparkling wine at parties. The sweetness of the dates plays nicely against the saltiness in the blue cheese to make a very sexy canape. They can be made a few hours in advance, just cover and keep refrigerated.

SHOPPING LIST

Blue cheese, 8 ounces
Select a sharp and fragrant blue cheese.

Greek style unflavored yogurt, 4 ounces

Medjool dates, 8 ounces (approximately 24 dates) You can usually find them in the dried fruit section of the supermarket.

EQUIPMENT

Food processor. (You can mix the mousse together by hand, but it will take a little effort)

Makes around 24 servings enough for 6 to 8 guests

In a food processor, blend the blue cheese and yogurt until very smooth. There should be very few lumps in the mixture. Season with salt and pepper, to taste.

Slice the dates lengthwise, cutting just deep enough to remove the pits. You do not want to cut all the way through the date. Spoon about ½ teaspoon of the cheese mixture into the cavity of the date, so the date is nice and full. Ideally your guests will bite into equal parts date and cheese mousse creating a perfectly balanced flavor explosion.

parmesan crisps with goat cheese and chive mousse

CHEESE-ON-CHEESE SUMS UP THESE TASTY morsels. There is great depth of flavor in this dish and it pairs equally well with red or white wine.

Preheat the oven 400° F and let the cream cheese come to room temperature.

To make the mousse, finely chop the chives. In a small bowl, mix together the goat cheese, cream cheese, heavy cream and chives. Add ground pepper and a small amount of salt to taste. The parmesan cheese is salty, so be careful not to add too much salt. It will take a little effort to get all the ingredients to blend together into a smooth mixture. You can make the goat cheese mousse up to 2 days in advance.

Next, prepare the crisps. Take the leaves of the thyme sprigs and finely chop the thyme leaves. In a separate bowl, mix together the parmesan cheese, flour and thyme.

On a baking sheet lined with a non-stick silicone pad or parchment paper, place a tablespoonful of the mixture and use your fingers to flatten it gently so it becomes a circle about 2 inches in diameter. Leave a couple inches between each mound as they spread during cooking. You should be able to fit 12 rounds on a baking sheet.

Makes approximately 30 servings

SHOPPING LIST

Goat cheese, 12 ounces

Cream cheese, 6 ounces

Chives, 2 ounces or 3 tablespoons

Heavy cream, 3 tablespoons

Finely shredded Parmesan cheese, 2 cups

All-purpose flour, 2 teaspoons

Fresh thyme, 3 sprigs

EQUIPMENT

Baking sheet

Non-stick silicone pad or parchment paper

Mixing bowls

Bake in the oven until the cheese melts and the edges just start to turn golden brown, 6 to 8 minutes. They can burn quickly so watch them carefully! When taking them out of the oven, let them cool for 5 minutes on the baking sheet before removing them to a plate and repeat until you have used up all of the parmesan cheese mixture. They will be fragile and pliable until they are completely cooled, about 20 minutes. The crisps can be made a few hours in advance, stored in an air-tight container. Separate the layers of crisps with wax paper so they do not stick to each other.

When the parmesan crisps are cooled and you are ready to serve, gently spoon a heaping tablespoon dollop of the goat cheese spread on top of each crisp.

Cheese and Wine Party

savory jam elephant ears (palmiers)

YOU HAVE PROBABLY SEEN THE classic sweet version of elephant ears, also known as palmiers. By using parmesan cheese instead of sugar and a jam that is not very sweet, it becomes the perfect accompaniment to sparkling wine. It is amazing how much punch you get from only 3 ingredients!

Defrost the frozen puff pastry; it will take about an hour sitting on the counter. It will become pliable, but still cold to the touch.

Preheat oven to 425° F. Line a baking sheet with silicone pad or parchment paper.

Sprinkle a thin layer of cheese on your cutting board or a work surface and cover it with a puff pastry sheet. Gently press down the pastry sheet so the cheese sticks to the bottom of it and smooth out the seams of the puff pastry sheet. Spread a VERY thin yet even layer of jam, leaving a one inch border along the edge. Fold in two opposite sides of the square so that the sides meet in the center. Fold in same sides of the pastry again to meet in center. It will look like a narrow rectangle with several layers and the cheese on the outside. Press down hard to help seal the seams, otherwise the pastry has a tendency to unfold while baking. Do not be surprised if a little jam oozes out.

Makes around 20 pieces

SHOPPING LIST

Frozen puff pastry, one package that contains 2 sheets

Jam*, 6 ounces

Parmesan cheese, 3 ounces

EQUIPMENT

Baking sheet

Silicone non-stick sheet or parchment pape

*Select a jam that is not too sweet, such as currant or spicy, hot pepper flavors. Avoid ones like Concord grape or strawberry.

Cut pastry crosswise into ½ inch-thick slices. Arrange with cut side down, on lined baking sheet. Repeat with remaining pastry sheet.

Bake palmiers in batches in middle of oven until golden brown, about 12 minutes. Transfer to a rack to cool completely. You can make these several hours in advance.

tarragon chicken skewers with pistachio cream sauce

THE CHICKEN IS EQUALLY DELICIOUS served warm or at room temperature. Both the chicken and sauce can be made in advance. Then just warm up the sauce when ready to serve. The bright and subtle flavors of tarragon chicken and cream sauce pair well with sparkling, white and rosé wines.

chicken skewers

Cut the chicken breasts into 1 inch cubes. Finely mince the garlic. Place the chicken and garlic in a plastic bag and add the lemon juice, olive oil and salt and pepper. Seal the plastic bag and let marinate in the refrigerator for 1 to 4 hours or even overnight.

Turn your oven to broil. Arrange the marinated chicken in a single layer on the baking sheets. Cook the chicken for 6 minutes. Flip over the chicken pieces and cook for another 6 minutes or until cooked through (no pink in the center). To serve, arrange the chicken pieces on a platter and skew each piece with a toothpick or skewer for easy dipping into the cream sauce.

Makes 6 servings

SHOPPING LIST – CHICKEN

Boneless skinless chicken breasts, two breasts, about 12 ounces

Tarragon, 2 tablespoons chopped

Lemon, 1 for juice

Garlic, one clove

Olive oil, 2 tablespoons

Salt, healthy pinch

Freshly ground pepper, 1/8 teaspoon

Salt and pepper to taste

pistachio cream sauce

Coarsely grind the pistachio nuts using a blender, immersion blender or food processor and set aside.

Heat olive oil in saucepan over medium heat and finely mince the shallot. Sauté the shallots until they are soft but not browned.

Add pistachios and cream; heat until the cream is warmed but not boiling. Add cheese and stir until the cheese is melted, the mixture is smooth and it is a creamy consistency. Add salt, pepper and red pepper to taste. The sauce can be made two days in advance and refrigerated. Just reheat before you are ready to serve.

SHOPPING LIST – SAUCE

Unsalted pistachio nuts, 1/4 cup ground coarsely (use blender)

Shallot, 1 chopped

Olive oil, 2 tablespoons

Heavy cream, 1/2 cup heavy cream

Parmigiano Reggiano, 1/2 cup

Salt, pepper and crushed red pepper to taste

EQUIPMENT

Bamboo skewers or long tooth picks

Baking sheet

Blender, immersion blender or food processor

balsamic chocolate truffles

CHOCOLATE TRUFFLES ARE THE PERFECT way to end a cheese and wine party. They pack a ton of flavor in a small bite that you can pop in your mouth. The addition of a little balsamic vinegar gives this dessert a subtle twist that your guests will love but struggle to identify. I have been known to bet a goodnight kiss if the most beautiful guest can guess the secret ingredient and she always ends up losing the bet. I secretly hope they know it is balsamic vinegar but want to lose the bet anyway. You can make them up to four days ahead; just keep them stored in a container with a tight lid.

Place one inch of water into the sauce pan and bring to a slow boil over medium heat. Place a heat resistant mixing bowl over the pan. The bowl should be big enough that it can sit over the sauce pan and the bottom does not touch the water.

Melt the chocolate along with the salt and cream in the mixing bowl over the simmering water. Make sure the mixing bowl is large enough to fit over the simmering water so that no steam or water condensation sneaks into the chocolate. If it does the water will ruin the chocolate. Once the chocolate is completely melted and the mixture is smooth, remove from heat. Stir in the balsamic vinegar. Pour the chocolate onto a baking sheet lined with parchment paper or wax paper and let cool in the refrigerator for at least 1 hour until firm.

SHOPPING LIST

High quality dark chocolate, 8 ½ ounces chopped

Cream, ¼ cup

Pinch of salt

Balsamic vinegar, 2 teaspoons

Unsweetened cocoa powder, ¼ cup

Confectioners' sugar, ¼ cup

EQUIPMENT

Sauce pot

Metal or glass mixing bowl that is heat resistant

Baking sheet

Wax paper or parchment paper

Take the truffle mixture from the refrigerator and shape the truffles by using a teaspoon to scoop out chocolate. With your fingertips shape into balls about the size of a cherry. If things start to get too messy, put the chocolate mixture back in the fridge for 15 minutes to chill and then continue.

Place the cocoa powder and confectioners' sugar in separate bowls. Place 6 truffles at a time in each of the bowls and roll the truffles around to coat entirely. Place the coated truffles on a large platter and continue with the remaining truffles. Use the different colored truffles to arrange them in an interesting pattern, be creative! If you made them ahead, store them in an airtight container in the refrigerator.

Cheese and Wine Party

culinary notes

culinary notes

5 THE INITIAL FLAME

... Pancetta wrapped shrimp with mustard wasabi dipping sauce

... Goat cheese quesadillas with watermelon salsa

... Sake and miso marinated skirt steak salad

... Grilled fruit and pound cake napoleon with berry sauce and tequila whipped cream

The Initial Flame

"Grilling takes the formality out of entertaining. Everyone wants to get involved."

Bobby Flay

Grilling basics for every gentlemen

a few basics every gentleman should know about grilling

KEEP YOUR GRILL CLEAN!

Always clean your grate immediately before and after cooking, using a long-handled stiff wire brush. It is easiest if you clean the grates after you finish cooking and they are still warm. If you cannot find your brush … which happens a lot to me … you can scour the grate with a ball of crumpled aluminum foil held in tongs.

KEEP YOUR GRATES LUBED

Use a tightly folded paper towel dipped in vegetable oil or a chunk of bacon fat held at the end of your tongs to oil the grate before you put on the food. Or do as Israeli grill masters do: Impale half an onion on the end of a barbecue fork. Dip the onion in oil and rub it across the bars of the grate.

TREAT YOUR FISH GENTLY

Don't turn the fish too early or too frequently. If you start with a clean grill that's heated properly, you should only have to turn your fish one time. Assuming your grill is hot enough, your fish may stick if you try to turn it too early. Give the fillets a few extra minutes to cook before trying to flip them again.

THINK ABOUT EVERYTHING YOU WILL NEED TO GRILL

Do not waste your time ducking in and out of the house for supplies. Arm yourself properly before you fire up the grill. That includes having enough beer for you to drink while cooking.

DON'T SLICE YOUR MEAT IN A HURRY

Even if you and your guests are starving, let your meat rest once it's cooked. The thicker the cut of meat, the longer it needs to rest – thin steaks rest 5 minutes, a whole pork butt rests 30.

AN INSTANT-READ THERMOMETER IS YOUR FRIEND.

Do not mutilate your meat trying to see if your steak is done.

INTERNAL TEMPERATURES FOR BEEF

    Rare – very red, cool center — 125° F

    Medium rare – red warm center — 135° F

    Medium – pink, hot center — 145° F

    Medium well – hint of pink hot center — 155° F

    Well Done – no pink, hot center — 165° F

pancetta wrapped shrimp with mustard wasabi dipping sauce

THIS IS HOW YOU CAN wow your guests with only five ingredients. You can prep this recipe in advance and grill the shrimp when you are ready to serve. The pancetta adds flavor and crispy texture while helping prevent the shrimp from being overcooked.

Makes 10-12 servings

Soak the skewers in water for at least an hour, this helps prevent them from burning during cooking.

Open beer and drink while you are grilling.

The shrimp should be shelled and deveined when you buy them. Wrap each shrimp tightly in a slice of pancetta. Skewer the shrimp, one per skewer.

Combine the Dijon mustard, crème fraiche and wasabi powder. Salt and pepper to taste and set aside in the refrigerator.

Start the grill and let it get hot. Lightly spray the pancetta wrapped shrimp with vegetable oil spray so they will not stick to the grill. Grill the shrimp on a hot grill for 2-3 minutes and when the pancetta starts to crisp, flip over to cook the other side. Continue grilling until the pancetta is crisp on all sides and the shrimp are just cooked through.

Place the cooked shrimp on a serving platter and serve with the dipping sauce.

SHOPPING LIST

Jumbo shrimp, 1 pound (size 10-15)

Pancetta, 12 very thin slices

Dijon mustard, 2 tablespoons

Crème fraiche, 4 tablespoons (can substitute sour cream)

Wasabi powder, 1 teaspoon

Beer, 1 bottle of your favorite (optional)

EQUIPMENT

Bamboo skewers

Vegetable oil spray

goat cheese quesadillas with watermelon salsa

THIS RECIPE IS A COOL twist on standard quesadillas and screams summer flavors. The watermelon salsa is good enough to eat a tub of by itself. Even folks who do not think they like goat cheese will love this dish.

Remove the seeds and finely mince the jalapeño peppers, mince ½ the red onion and chop the leaves from 4 or 5 sprigs of fresh mint. Finely chop ½ the English cucumber. If you cannot find an English cucumber, buy a regular one and remove the seeds before chopping. In a small bowl, add the juice of the lemon and lime. Add the cucumber, cubed watermelon, jalapeño pepper, onion, mint, honey, and olive oil and toss to blend. Season with salt and pepper to taste. Cover and refrigerate at least 30 minutes. (Can be prepared 2 hours ahead).

Start the grill and let it get hot. Place 2 tablespoons (1 ounce) of goat cheese in the middle of each tortilla and fold in half. Gently push down to help the goat cheese spread out evenly. Repeat with all of the tortillas.

Spray both sides of the tortillas with the non-stick vegetable spray. Cook about 3 minutes, until the bottom turns golden brown. Turn the quesadilla over and continue cooking, about 3 minutes more, until the other side is golden brown and the cheese is melted. Remove from the grill and cut into wedges. Top with salsa and serve immediately.

Makes 10 servings

If you want to make this more of an entrée-type dish, add a few pieces of cooked shrimp to the goat cheese and then grill.

SHOPPING LIST

10-inch flour tortillas, 10

Goat cheese, 10 ounces

Lime, 1

Lemon, 1

Seedless watermelon, about ½ a medium size, enough to give you 2 cups of ½-inch cubes

English cucumber, 1

Red onion, 1 small

Jalapeño peppers, 2

Honey, 1 teaspoon

Olive oil, ⅓ cup

Fresh mint, a few sprigs

EQUIPMENT

Olive oil spray or non-stick cooking spray

Mixing bowl

Tongs

sake and miso marinated skirt steak salad

THERE IS A LOT TO love about this salad. The marinade imparts tons of flavor to the meat and the salad has a nice variety of colors and textures. Since men want to eat steaks and women want to have salads, it is one of those rare salads that both men and women will find satisfying. Most major supermarkets now have a large selection of Asian products and there you can probably find all of the ingredients you need. Letting the steak marinate overnight will make the steak unforgettable.

marinade

Roughly chop up the lemongrass and garlic. In a mixing bowl combine the garlic, lemongrass, red miso, vegetable oil, and ginger powder. Put the steak and the marinade in resealable plastic bag and marinate in the refrigerator for 12-24 hours.

dressing

Mince the mint leaves from the 4 sprigs. Whisk together the vinegar, 1 tablespoon sake, mint leaves, mustard and juice from lemon in small bowl to blend. Gradually whisk in oil. Season to taste with salt and pepper.

Cut the cucumbers in half and slice thinly. Cut the olives in half and slice the onion into very thin slices. Drain the canned corn and rinse the tomatoes. Cut the bottom stem off the romaine lettuce and cut into 1 inch pieces – or buy pre-washed lettuce.

Heat the grill pan over high heat. Grill the steak, about 4-6 minutes on each side for medium. The time will depend on the thickness of the steak and temperature of the pan. Let rest for 10 minutes on the cutting board. Cut the steak into thin strips ACROSS the grain. If you cut along the grain, the meat will be stringy and tough. In cuts of meat like the flank steak, the grain is clearly visible. It is the lines running across the steak.

Makes 8-10 servings

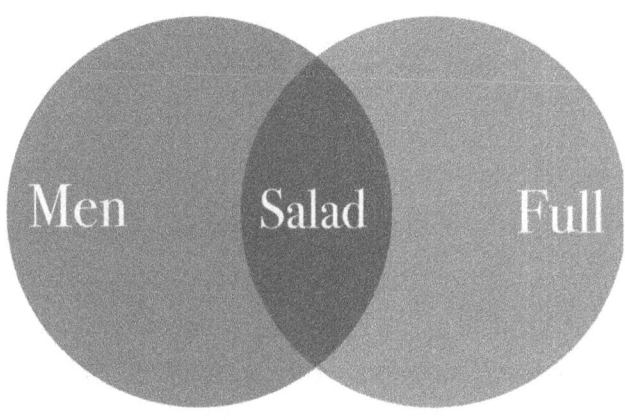

ASSEMBLY

On a large platter, spread out the arugula and romaine. Drizzle half of the salad dressing over the lettuce and gently toss. Artistically (or as close as you can get) spread the tomatoes, olives, red onions and corn over the lettuce. Lay the sliced steak over the salad and drizzle with the remaining salad dressing.

The Initial Flame

SHOPPING LIST

Sake, 2 cups plus 1 tablespoon

Red miso, 1 cup (found in Asian grocery stores)

Vegetable oil, 1 cup

Lemongrass, one 14-inch piece (optional)

Garlic, 4 cloves

Ginger powder, 2 teaspoons

Skirt steak, 2 pounds

Arugula, 6 cups (about 12 ounces)

Romaine lettuce, 2 bunches

English cucumbers, 2

Cherry tomatoes, 1 pint (around 24)

Kalamata olives or other brine-cured black olives, 2 cups. Buy ones that are pitted!

Red onion, 1

Mint, 4 sprigs 2 tablespoons

Corn, 1 small can (15 ounces)

Extra virgin Olive oil, 1 cup

Sherry wine vinegar, 4 tablespoons

Dijon mustard, 2 teaspoons

Lemons, 2

EQUIPMENT

Grill pan or large skillet

Very large platter

grilled fruit and pound cake napoleon with berry sauce and tequila whipped cream

THIS COLORFUL DISH HAS EVERYTHING you want in a summer dessert—seasonal fruit, rich pound cake and alcohol spiked whipped cream. You can substitute different fruit, based on what is in season and looks great in your local market. If you have a guest who will be spending the night, you can make a little extra tequila whipped cream for post party activities.

Using a small sauce pan over low heat, empty both jars of fruit preserves and warm the preserves.

Cut the banana into thick slices on the diagonal, at least 1 inch thick. If the banana slices are too thin then they could fall apart during the grilling. Cut peaches into halves, carving around the pit if needed. Coat all of the fruit with the vegetable oil so they don't stick to the grates and lightly season with salt.

If you have already been using the grill for your entrees, then carefully clean the grill before you start cooking the fruit. You do not want meat residue finding its way into your dessert.

Over high heat, grill all of the fruit for 2-3 minutes per side. Distinctive grill marks should develop and the fruit begins to soften. You do not want the fruit to get mushy! After the fruit is grilled, slice each pound cake into 8 slices. Coat the cake with oil on both sides. Grill the pound cake for 1-2 minutes per side, so they develop grill marks. Be gentle with the cake since it can be fragile.

Makes 8-10 servings

ASSEMBLY

Coat 8 slices of pound cake with half of the mascarpone cheese and lay the slices on the platter. Spread half of the fruit over the cake and drizzle with ½ of the warmed preserves. Top with the remaining pound cake, mascarpone cheese, grilled fruit and warmed preserves.

Using a mixer, whip the cream, sugar and tequila until the cream thickens and has the texture you prefer in whipped cream. Top the dessert with the whipped cream and add a few basil leaves as garnish.

SHOPPING LIST

Heavy cream, 1 cup

2 tablespoons of tequila
(Silver or Blanco)

4 tablespoons of confectioners'
(powdered) sugar

Peaches, 6
(can substitute plums or nectarines)

Bananas, 4

Pound cake, 2
You can use any brand easily found in your local supermarket.

Mascarpone cheese, 8 ounces

Jar of your favorite fruit preserves, 2
13-ounce jars

Vegetable oil, ¾ cup

Basil leaves for garnish

EQUIPMENT

Small sauce pan

Stand mixer or immersion mixer

Large plate for serving

culinary notes

culinary notes

The Initial Flame

POOL PARTY 6

- Cold melon soup shooters with prosciutto salt
- Drunken pineapple rum shrimp ceviche
- Cobb salad sandwiches
- Lamb sliders with mint yogurt sauce and homemade pickled onions

IF YOU AND FRIENDS ARE sitting by the pool, then it is obviously hot outside and you only want to serve light and refreshing food. To me that screams fresh seasonal fruit, which is reflected in several of these recipes. It is more than acceptable to use paper plates, plastic cups, etc., around the pool. You should not even think about using glass poolside.

You will want to have a lot of bottled water, plan on at least one small bottle of water per guest per hour. Always buy one more bag of ice than you think you will need, because you will use every last cube.

Beer, white wine and soda will be the drinks of choice but having a big pitcher of Sangria is not a bad idea either. My recipe includes a lot of fruit, so it is almost like a health drink.

ultimate sangria

SHOPPING LIST

Two bottles dry red wine

⅔ cup brandy

1 cup Cointreau or triple sec

1 cup pomegranate liquor (the secret weapon)

1 small lemon, thinly sliced crosswise

2 medium pear, diced

2 medium apples

1 cup of fresh berries such as raspberries, blueberries, etc.

12 ounces ginger ale

Mix together all of the alcohol and fruit. Refrigerate until cold and add the ginger ale just as you are ready to serve.

cold melon soup shooters with prosciutto salt

FEW THINGS ARE AS REFRESHING on a hot summer day as a cold melon soup. Serve it in small glasses and spoons are rendered unnecessary. What makes this recipe special is the prosciutto salt, which is easy to make and adds great texture and a salty touch. This dish is best made a few hours in advance and put in the fridge to chill.

prosciutto salt

Place the prosciutto slices on top of each other and finely mince them.

Heat a saute pan over medium high heat with the tablespoon of oil. Saute the prosciutto pieces until they become very crispy and slightly darker in color. Using a slotted spoon remove the cooked prosciutto and place on a plate lined with a paper towel to drain and cool. You can make this a day in advance, just store in a sealed container or plastic bag.

melon soup

When you buy the cantaloupe you want to find ones that are very ripe. They will have a sweet smell and be slightly soft to the touch. If the melons are ripe enough, you can remove the seeds and then scoop out the flesh of the melon. Two cantaloupes should give you around 4 to 5 cups of flesh.

Makes 8-10 shooters

Put cantaloupe flesh into a blender or food processor along with the wine blend until very smooth. If it does not all fit into the blender, then do in two batches. Pour into a large mixing bowl and add the honey, lime juice, nutmeg, salt and cayenne and blend until well mixed. Depending on the ripeness of the melon, you might want to add a little more honey to taste. Place in the refrigerator for at least 2 hours, until nice and cold.

When ready to serve, pour into small glasses and garnish with some prosciutto salt and a mint leaf.

SHOPPING LIST

Cantaloupes, 2 medium size

Fruity white wine, like a Riesling or Chenin Blanc, 1 cup

Honey, 1 tablespoon

Lime, one for juice

Nutmeg ¼ teaspoon

Salt, ¼ teaspoon

Cayenne, generous pinch

Fresh mint, for garnish

Prosciutto, 3 slices
   Ask the deli to slice the prosciutto slightly thicker than they usually do.

Vegetable oil, 1 tablespoon

EQUIPMENT

Blender or food processor

Large mixing bowl

Small saute pan

Slotted spoon

drunken pineapple rum shrimp ceviche

CEVICHE IS A SPICY LATIN American seafood dish that can be an appetizer, first course or just an amazing snack. It's claim to fame is that it's not cooked with heat, but by the acidity in citrus juices as it sits in the refrigerator. This dish seems to have a lot of ingredients, but the contrast in colors, tastes and textures is what makes it addictive. Start to make this dish 5-7 hours or even overnight before you plan on serving.

DO AHEAD

Cut each shrimp in half and place back in the refrigerator. Clean the cutting board and dice the red bell pepper. The pepper pieces should be the same size or smaller than the shrimp pieces. Mince the shallot into small pieces and finely mince the jalapeño peppers. The heat of the jalapeño adds a lot to the dish, but you do not want your guest biting into a huge chunk of the pepper

Open the can of pineapple slices and reserve the juice. Cut the pineapple slices into pieces the same size as the shrimp pieces. Mince the garlic clove.

Place the shrimp in a glass dish with the lime juice, orange juice, reserved pineapple juice, bell pepper, shallot, rum, jalapeño pepper, salt, garlic, and ginger powder, tossing to coat. All of the shrimp should be covered by liquid, add more orange juice if needed. Cover and refrigerate for 5 to 7 hours or even overnight, until shrimp are "cooked" to your desired degree, stirring the mixture every hour or so.

Makes 6 appetizer portions

WHEN READY TO SERVE

Drain off most of the liquid and add the chopped cilantro and olive oil. Add additional salt to taste if necessary. Serve the ceviche in a large bowl surrounded by tortilla chips.

If you procrastinated and do not have several hours for this dish to "cook" in the refrigerator, then cut the shrimp into smaller pieces. The greater surface area will accelerate the process.

SHOPPING LIST

Very fresh shrimp, 1 pound (31-40 size is a good size to use), shelled and deveined

Limes, 2

Orange juice, ½ cup

Red bell pepper, 1

Shallot, 1 medium

Pineapple, 20 ounce can sliced

Dark rum, 3 tablespoons

Jalapeño peppers, 2

Garlic, one clove minced

Ginger powder, 1 tablespoon

Fresh cilantro leaves, ¼ cup chopped

Good quality extra-virgin olive oil, 2 tablespoons

Salt, ½ tablespoon

Tortilla chips

EQUIPMENT

Glass bowl

cobb salad sandwiches

THE INSPIRATION FOR THIS SANDWICH is the Cobb Salad, made famous in the Brown Derby restaurant during the 1930s. The secret to this recipe is to have the bacon, eggs and chicken cooked in advance. All you have to do at the last minute is mix up the avocado-blue cheese mixture, toast the bread and assemble the sandwich.

In a medium size sauce pan over low heat poach the chicken breasts in enough water to just cover the chicken. The water should be barely boiling and add a pinch of salt and pepper to the water. It should take around 20 minutes for the chicken to be fully cooked. Let cool and slice each breast piece into about 5 thick slices. Can be done a day in advance, store in the refrigerator.

Place the bacon on a sheet rack and bake in a 350 degree oven. It will take around 20-30 minutes for the bacon to be done to the crispiness of your choosing. You can also cook the bacon in a frying pan on the stove, but that makes more of a mess to clean up than cooking it in the oven. The bacon can be cooked a few hours in advance.

To hard boil the eggs, put them in a sauce pan with enough water to cover the eggs. Turn the heat on to medium high and when the water reaches a boil, turn off the heat and cover. After 10 minutes, take the eggs out and put into a bowl full of ice water. When the eggs are cool enough to easily work with, peel and set aside. Can be done a day in advance, store in the refrigerator.

Makes 4 sandwiches

Just before you are ready to serve, toast the bread. If you have unsliced bread, using a serrated knife, cut the bread into thick slices about ¾ of an inch.

Set out a mixing bowl. Cut the avocados in half, discard the pit and scoop the flesh into the bowl. Add 6 ounces of blue cheese, one tablespoon of Dijon mustard and mix well. You want to mash up the avocados and have the entire mixture be an almost smooth paste. Season with salt and pepper to taste.

For each sandwich, spread the avocado-blue cheese mixture on both sides of the toast. Add ¼ of the chicken, 1 egg cut into thick slices, 2 pieces of bacon and two tomato slices. This will be a THICK sandwich, be careful when you cut it in half to serve.

SHOPPING LIST

Avocados, 3 – they should be very ripe.*

Blue cheese, 6 ounces - a nice assertive one like Roquefort works well

Dijon mustard

Bacon, 8 slices or about ½ pound

Eggs, 4

A loaf of good quality white bread, preferably unsliced or 4 rolls

Whole skinless boneless chicken breasts, 2 (can substitute 1 pound of sliced turkey breast)

Tomatoes, 2, sliced

EQUIPMENT

Medium size sauce pan

Baking sheet (if you line it with aluminum foil, it will be easier to clean)

When buying avocados there is an easy way to check ripeness. If you flick the small stem it should come off easily and you will see green underneath with ripe ones. If the stem does not come off easily or you see brown underneath, the avocado is not ripe.

Pool Party

lamb sliders with mint yogurt sauce and homemade pickled onions

THE PICKLED ONIONS ARE WHAT bring this dish together. In addition to the acidic bite that works well with the richness of the lamb and the creaminess of the sauce, the red pickled onion adds a tremendous visual pop to the plate. They can be made up to two weeks in advance and leftover pickled onions make a welcome addition to any sandwich you make.

pickled onions

SHOPPING LIST

Red onions, 2 large

Red wine vinegar, 3 cups

Olive oil, ¼ cup

Sugar, 2 tablespoons

Garlic, 2 cloves

Whole black peppercorns, 6 (or ½ teaspoon of ground pepper)

Fresh thyme, 4 sprigs

Salt, 1 tablespoon

DO AHEAD

You want to pickle the onions in advance, anywhere from overnight to 2 weeks prior to serving.

Peel and cut the onion in half. Slice the onions as thinly as you possibly can and set aside.

Place the vinegar, olive oil, sugar, peppercorns, garlic, salt and thyme in a large saucepan and bring to a boil. Stir until the sugar is dissolved. Turn off the heat and add the sliced onions to the hot liquid and steep for 15 minutes. When cool enough to work with, place in a container with a tight fitting lid and refrigerate for at least 2 hours or overnight. When ready to serve, drain the pickled onions from the liquid.

Makes 6-8 sliders

lamb sliders and yogurt sauce

Preheat oven to 400° F.

Mince one cup of mint leaves and the garlic clove. Juice the lemon and set aside the juice.

In a mixing bowl, whisk together yogurt, minced mint, ouzo, lemon juice and minced garlic. Salt and pepper to taste.

Finely mince the shallot.

Mix the lamb, shallot, salt, pepper, and allspice with your hands in a bowl until just combined (do not overwork mixture or the patties will become tough). Form into 8 small patties about ½ inch thick and set aside. Ideally the patties will be about the same size as the diameter of the French or Italian bread.

Either grill or cook the patties in the pan over medium high heat for about 4 minutes per side. They should have a developed a nice crust but still be slightly pink in the middle. Let them rest for 10 minutes after you take them out of the pan.

While the lamb is resting, prepare the toast. Cut the bread into thick slices, about ½ inch thick. Brush both sides of bread slices lightly with the oil and place on a baking sheet. Toast in the oven for about 10 minutes until golden, turning once.

Place the lamb burgers on toast pieces, then spoon sauce over and top with pickled onions and top with another piece of toast.

SHOPPING LIST

Plain Greek style yogurt, 1 cup

Whole fresh mint, one bunch 1 cup loosely packed leaves plus 2 tablespoons minced

Lemon, 1 small, juiced

Ouzo 1 teaspoon (optional)

Garlic, 1 clove, halved lengthwise

Ground lamb, 1 ½ pounds

Shallot, 1 medium

Salt, ¾ teaspoon

Black pepper, ½ teaspoon

Ground allspice, ¼ teaspoon

Olive oil, 2 ounces

One loaf of thick French or Italian bread

EQUIPMENT

Cast iron skillet or thick bottom pan. You can also fire up the grill

2 mixing bowls

Baking sheet

culinary notes

culinary notes

Pool Party

TAILGATING IN STYLE

- Grilled vegetable antipasto with herb goat cheese on crostini
- Chili rubbed beef tenderloin sliders with cilantro lime mayo
- Roasted corn salad
- S'mores bars

A GREAT TAILGATE PARTY REQUIRES a little extra planning since you are going to be in a parking lot, not your kitchen.

Know the local rules. Most stadiums have strict rules about when, where, and how people can tailgate. Do not even think about bringing alcohol if you are going to watch a high school game.

You do not want to miss the game so budget time for these basic (but often overlooked) party-time tasks:

- Hauling and setting up tables and chairs: *20 minutes*
- Preheating the grill: *30 minutes for charcoal, 20 minutes for gas*
- Bathroom run: *20 minutes*
- Cleanup: *15 minutes*
- Finding the nearest garbage can with room for all your post-party trash: *30 minutes.*

A gentleman never leaves behind a mess. That includes putting any leftovers you plan on keeping in cold storage, throwing away your trash and safely disposing of any hot coals from your grill.

Bring twice as many paper towels, plastic garbage bags and wet wipes as you think you need.

grilled vegetable antipasto with goat cheese on crostini

THIS DISH IS EASY TO cook ahead of time and bring to the game. It is a healthy and light way to start off the tailgate.

dressing

Mince the garlic and combine with the balsamic vinegar, red wine vinegar, dried basil, oregano and red pepper flakes. I like the depth of flavor that using two different vinegars has. It makes a big difference in the dish. Slowly whisk in a half cup of olive oil and set aside.

Cut the fennel crosswise into ¼ inch slices. Cut the red bell pepper into thin strips and cut the zucchinis into long thin strips. You want to try and have the vegetable slices about the same thickness. Lightly coat cut vegetables with ½ cup of vegetable oil and sprinkle with salt. One by one lay the vegetable slices on a grill over direct medium heat. If you do not have a grill, cook the vegetables using your broiler. Cook about 5 minutes. Turn the vegetables over and cook 3 or 4 minutes longer. As soon as vegetables are done, remove from grill and transfer to a platter. Cut the vegetables into a medium dice, the pieces should be around the size of an M&M candy. While the vegetables are still warm add ½ the dressing and let cool to room temperature. Adding the dressing while the vegetable are still warm will help them absorb the dressing. Cut the soppressata and olives into pieces around the same size as the vegetables. Add balance of the dressing and set aside.

Makes 10 servings

Preheat oven to 350° F.

Cut the baguette into ½ inch slices. Put the bread slices on a baking sheet and brush slices with 2 tablespoons of olive oil. Season lightly with salt and pepper, then bake until pale golden, about 10 minutes. Let cool.

Store the vegetable mixture, cheese and toasted baguette slices separately to bring to the game.

At the game, smear a small amount of the goat cheese on each piece of toasted baguette and then, using a slotted spoon, add a heaping tablespoon of the antipasto on top.

SHOPPING LIST

Garlic, 2 cloves

Balsamic vinegar, 3 tablespoons

Red-wine vinegar, 2 tablespoons

Dried basil, 1 teaspoon

Dried oregano, 1 teaspoon

Dried hot red pepper flakes, ¼ teaspoon

Olive oil, ½ cup plus 2 tablespoons

Vegetable oil, ½ cup

Fennel bulbs, 2 small (about 1 ½ pounds)

Red bell peppers, 3 medium size

Large zucchinis or summer squash, 2 medium size

Black or green brine-cured olives, ¾ pound

Soppressata, ½ pound (can substitute salami)

Goat cheese, 6 ounces

Baguette, 1

EQUIPMENT

Mixing bowl

Baking sheet

Whisk

Grill

Tailgating in Style

chili rubbed beef tenderloin sliders with cilantro lime mayo

THESE ARE SO GOOD THAT often folks tailgating around us offer to buy sliders off of us. Of course my friends and I say "NO" as we inhale these awesome, flavor packed little bites. You can taste the difference when you make your own spice rub, but you can buy a packed spice rub as a shortcut. Try to find a market that sells spices in bulk so you purchase only the amount you need.

You can make the cilantro lime mayonnaise up to two days in advance, coat the tenderloin with the spice rub the night before the game and then just grill the tenderloin at the tailgate.

In a food processor, blend Dijon mustard, garlic cloves, leaves from half of the cilantro bunch, juice from 2 limes and process until cilantro and garlic are finely chopped. Add mayonnaise and process just until blended. Season with salt and pepper to taste. Set aside in the refrigerator.

DO IN ADVANCE

Stir together chili rub ingredients in a small bowl; ancho, cayenne, espresso, garlic, dry mustard, brown sugar, salt and pepper. You can make the spice run a day in advance. The night before the game you can prep the tenderloin. Make sure the tenderloin is trimmed of silver skin, that white almost silver very thin membrane. It is inedible and would ruin the texture of the sandwich. Generously coat the meat with the spice rub and press it into the meat. Do this the night before and refrigerate the tenderloin.

Makes 10-12 servings

AT THE GAME

Set up the grill and arrange the charcoals so there will be a hot area and a cooler area of the grill. An easy way to bring the oil to the game to prep the grill grates is to soak a paper towel in the oil and pack it in a small plastic bag. Lightly oil the grates so the tenderloin will not stick. When the charcoals are ready, sear the beef directly over hottest part of grill, turning occasionally, until well browned, 12 to 15 minutes total. Move beef to coolest part of grill, then cover the grill, turning occasionally, until thermometer inserted diagonally into center registers 120° F for medium-rare, about 10 minutes. If your grill does not have a lid you can use an inverted disposable roasting pan to cover the meat.

Transfer beef to a cutting board and let rest for 20 minutes. Cut the beef into thin slices. Assemble sandwiches with a generous dollop of the cilantro-lime mayonnaise.

SHOPPING LIST

Ancho chili powder, 1 ½ teaspoons

Cayenne chili powder, 1 teaspoon

Fine ground espresso coffee, 1 ½ teaspoons

Brown sugar, 1 teaspoon

Dry mustard, ¼ teaspoon

Granulated garlic, 1 teaspoon

Salt, 1 teaspoon

Black pepper ½ teaspoon

Center cut beef tenderloin, 3 pounds

Small rolls, 20-24 (Silver dollar dinner rolls, mini-Hawaiian rolls or any soft crust small roll)

Limes, 2 for juice

Garlic, 2 cloves

Hot sauce

Dijon mustard, 1 teaspoon

Cilantro, 1 bunch

Mayonnaise, 1 cup

Vegetable oil, 1 tablespoon

EQUIPMENT

Grill – bring to the game

Food processor

Instant read thermometer – bring to the game

Plastic cutting board – bring to the game

Sharp knife – bring to the game

Tailgating in Style

roasted corn salad

THIS IS THE PERFECT SALAD to bring to the game. It's easy to make, has tons of flavor and looks great on the plate. You can make it the day before and bring to the game and enjoy at room temperature.

Makes 10 servings

SHOPPING LIST

Corn still in the husks, 8 ears

Red bell pepper, 1

Serrano peppers, 2

Red onion, 1 small

Fresh cilantro, 1 bunch

Olive oil, ½ cup

Garlic, 4 cloves

Limes, 3 for juice

Honey, 1 teaspoon

Queso cotija cheese, ¼ pound (can substitute Feta cheese)

EQUIPMENT

Mixing bowl

Tongs

Food processor

Preheat the oven to 400° F.

In a large pot or in the sink, soak the corn for 15 minutes. The moisture in the husk will create steam during the cooking and help the corn cook evenly.

Put the corn directly on the racks in the oven and cook for 20 minutes or until tender.

While the corn is cooking, finely dice the Serrano peppers and dice the red bell pepper, set aside.

FOR THE DRESSING

In a blender or food processor, mix cilantro leaves from half the bunch, olive oil, garlic, lime juice, honey, salt and pepper. Blend until smooth and set aside.

Use tongs to remove the corn from the oven. When cool enough to handle, remove the husks and silk from the corn. Cut the corn kernels from the cob, and place in a medium bowl. Mix in the red bell pepper, Serrano peppers and red onion. Stir in the dressing and mix to coat the corn and peppers evenly.

Garnish with queso cotija cheese (or feta) and serve at room temperature.

s'mores bars

I LOVE THIS MAKE AHEAD dessert, it combines all the flavors of the classic s'mores dessert in an easy to transport method. The hardest part of this recipe is not finishing them all before the game!

Makes 10-12 servings

Preheat the oven to 350° F.

Melt the butter in the microwave. In a bowl combine well the crumbs, the sugar, the salt, and the butter. Reserving 1 cup of the mixture, firmly press the remaining mixture into the bottom of a 13 x 9 inch baking dish. Bake the crust in the oven for 12 minutes or until it begins to turn golden. Let the crust cool in the dish.

Preheat the broiler.

In a metal bowl set over a saucepan of barely simmering water, melt the chocolate, stirring often. Pour melted chocolate over the crust spreading it evenly, and sprinkle it with the marshmallows, pressing them lightly so the marshmallows set into the chocolate. Sprinkle the reserved crumb mixture over the top. Broil the dessert under a preheated broiler about 2 inches from the heat for 30 seconds, or until the marshmallows melt and begin to brown. Let it cool completely and cut it into squares to bring to the game.

SHOPPING LIST

Graham cracker crumbs, 2 ¼ cups (one box of crackers)

Sugar, ⅓ cup

Salt, ¼ teaspoon

Butter, 1 stick (½ cup)

Dark or bittersweet chocolate, 1 pound

Mini-marshmallows, 4 cups

EQUIPMENT

13 x 9 inch baking dish

Mixing bowl

culinary notes

culinary notes

8 OCTOBERFEST

... Bratwurst patty sandwiches on pretzel rolls

... Bratkartoffeln (Fried potatoes laced with bacon and onions)

... Schnitzel with baked apples stuffed with spicy red cabbage

... Apple Gingerbread bread pudding

NOT WANTING TO BUY TICKETS to Munich for the celebrated two week drinking and eating festival is no reason not to celebrate. You never need a reason to invite friends over to enjoy great beer and food.

Primer on some of the most popular German beers:

Berliner Weisse	A wheat beer with a low alcohol content.
Bock	Think of bock as you would a traditional English stout: very dark amber to dark brown color with a lot of malt and very little hops, so it isn't bitter.
Munich Dunkel	Another medium-bodied, darker German brew that features a low to moderate alcohol content. It generally tastes of toasted chocolate.
Weizenbier	A light- to medium-bodied wheat beer with little hops.
Märzen	A medium-bodied Munich lager with a good balance of bitterness and nice, malty sweetness. Märzen is generally an amber to deep copper color.
Helles	This mildly hopped, malty beer from Munich is pale to golden in color with a caramel sweetness.
Pils	Pilsner has a flowery, medium-hop bouquet with a nice, dry, crisp flavor and a light to medium body.

homemade bratwurst patty sandwiches on pretzel rolls

IT IS RARE FOR ME to bake, especially a recipe that involves two cooking steps, but these rolls are special. They are perfect for brats, but will make almost any sandwich better. Once you make your own bratwurst sausage and rolls for parties your guests will start inviting themselves back over and over. It is best if the rolls are made the day you will serve them, but they also store well in the freezer. The salt topping will become soggy after a day.

(for bratwurst patties, see page 104)

pretzel rolls

For the pretzel rolls, a proper crust is what separates a good roll from a great roll so it is worth the extra step or two.

Measure 1 ½ cups of warm water (110°F or comfortably warm to the touch). You can use hot water from the sink. It should feel warm but not hot. Combine with the yeast package into the bowl of the mixer. After about 5 minutes you will see foam starting to form on the surface. If you do not see any foam, then the yeast is not working and you have to start over. The water might have been too hot.

Melt the butter in the microwave. In the stand mixer bowl add the yeasty water, melted butter along with the sugar, flour and salt and mix until thoroughly combined. The dough comes together and should be smooth, but not very sticky, to the touch. It helps if you have a dough hook to use, but the standard paddle that came with the mixer works fine. Cover with a towel and let rise for one hour or until doubled in bulk. Ideally, you want to do this in a space in your kitchen that is not near an air conditioning vent or breezes.

Have a work space ready for you to play with your dough, either a cutting board or any smooth surface. Lightly dust the work area with flour and turn out the dough from the bowl. Push the dough down a little bit so that it is easier to work with.

Makes 12 small sandwiches or 6 BIG sandwiches

Cut the dough into 12 pieces and form into balls. Shaping the rolls will take a little practice. Take a piece of dough and start forming a nice round, smooth ball by pulling the sides to the center and squeezing the bottom to seal. You should be creating a smooth skin on the surface of the dough ball. Think of how you want the final roll to look and use that image of the taut dark brown exterior to help you when shaping the rolls.

Space the rolls evenly on the prepared sheet pan, seam side down, leaving a little room between each roll. Cover with a towel and let rise for 30 minutes or until the rolls have doubled in size.

Preheat oven to 425° F.

In the large saucepan or pot bring two quarts of water to a slow boil. Add the baking soda and lower heat so the water is barely simmering.

Place a few of the rolls into the simmering water with the seam side down. After a minute, flip so the other side of the roll can cook for a minute. Remove with a slotted spoon and place back on the lined baking sheet with the seam side down. Repeat until all of the rolls are done. This poaching step is what gives the pretzels their unique and firm crust.

In a small bowl beat the egg. Using your finger (or a pastry brush) coat each roll with the egg wash and top with coarse salt. Using a sharp knife, cut a slash on the top of each roll. You do not have go deep, maybe a ¼ of an inch deep.

Bake the rolls for 15-20 minutes. When they are starting to brown, turn on the broiler so that the pretzels develop a dark brown surface. Watch carefully during this step since they can burn easily.

PRETZEL ROLLS SHOPPING LIST

Active dry yeast, one small

Sugar, 2 teaspoons

All-purpose flour, 4 ½ cups

Kosher salt, 2 teaspoons

Butter, 4 Tablespoons

Baking soda ¼ cup

Egg, 1 large

Large grain salt, like sea salt

EQUIPMENT

Large pot or sauce pan

Baking sheet

Silicone non-stick pad or parchment paper

Stand mixer

Hand towel

Slotted spoon

bratwurst patties

SHOPPING LIST

Ground pork, 2 ½ pounds

Dried sage, 2 teaspoons

Salt, 2 teaspoons

Ground black pepper, 1 teaspoon

Dry mustard, ½ teaspoon

Nutmeg, ½ teaspoon

Sugar, 1 teaspoon

Worcestershire sauce, a few splashes

Lager beer, 4 ounces

Spicy German style mustard, a small jar

Vegetable oil, 1 tablespoon

EQUIPMENT

Large non-stick sauté pan

In a large bowl thoroughly mix the pork, sage, salt, pepper, mustard, nutmeg, sugar, Worcestershire, and beer. Use your hands; just make sure you wash them before and after!

It helps to do this the night before and store in the refrigerator so the spices can fully flavor the pork. If you don't have time to soak the pork then it is fine to cook it right after mixing it all together.

Form patties that are approximately 2-inch round or whatever size you made the pretzel rolls.

Heat a large non-stick skillet over medium heat with the oil. Cook the patties for around 5-6 minutes on each side. They should be browned on both sides. The bratwurst patties will be cooked medium, slightly pink in the center and very moist. Let the patties rest for 2-3 minutes. Serve on the pretzel rolls with mustard.

bratkartofflen (fried potatoes laced with bacon and onions)

THIS DISH IS ONE OF my guilty pleasures. It is a perfect complement to sausages, schnitzel, grilled steak or almost anything except ice cream. I know I say this recipe makes 6-8 servings, but I am not too embarrassed to admit I have eaten almost the entire dish as my supper occasionally.

Roughly chop the potatoes into large cubes, about the size of a pair of dice. Put the potato cubes in a pot and fill with cold water until the water just covers the potatoes. Boil potatoes in their skin until just tender, but still firm. You do not want to overcook them to the point they are falling apart. This can be done a day in advance and refrigerate the potatoes.

Dice and gently sauté bacon in a large frying pan until fully cooked and crisp. While bacon is cooking, thinly slice the onions. Remove crisp bacon and set aside. Add the diced onions into the bacon drippings in the pan. Sauté the onions over low heat until the onion slices begin to brown, 15-20 minutes. Remove the onions from the pan and set aside with the crisp bacon.

Do not drain any remaining bacon drippings from the pan; this is what adds flavor to the dish. Add the vegetable oil to the bacon drippings and heat over medium-high. Add the cubed potatoes to the pan. Sprinkle with salt and pepper and sauté the potatoes until they begin to turn golden brown. Return the bacon and onions to the pan and toss gently with the potatoes. Sauté over medium low heat for another 5 minutes. Taste and add more salt and pepper, if desired. Place into a serving bowl.

Serves 6-8

SHOPPING LIST

Potatoes 5 pounds – Yukon gold

Bacon, 8 ounces

Yellow onions, 2 (can substitute white onion or sweet onion)

Vegetable oil, ½ cup

Pepper, ½ teaspoon

Salt, 1 teaspoon

EQUIPMENT

Large sauté pan

Pot to boil potatoes

Slotted spoon

schnitzel with baked apples stuffed with spicy red cabbage

THROUGHOUT MY TRAVELS TO AUSTRIA and Central Europe, Wiener Schnitzel is one of my favorite dishes and I have ordered it countless times. I was stunned to learn how easy it is to replicate at home. This dish has wonderful balance between the crunch and richness of the schnitzel and the sweetness and earthiness of the apple with cabbage.

schnitzel

Place a cutlet between two sheets of plastic wrap and use a heavy flat bottom pan to pound the meat. You want to pound it very thin, about ¼ inch thickness. Repeat for the other cutlets.

Set up the 3 shallow bowls. Place the flour with salt and pepper in one and breadcrumbs in another. Beat the eggs in the third bowl. Pour enough oil in the pan that it comes up at least ½ inch in the pan and heat over medium high. The oil should get very hot and the surface should begin to shimmer. To test if it is hot enough, immediately drop a few crumbs into the oil and they should begin to sizzle.

Working one at a time, dredge cutlets first in flour until the surface is evenly coated. Dip in egg to coat; allow the excess to drip off for a few seconds and then roll quickly in the breadcrumbs until coated. Do not press breadcrumbs into the meat. Immediatelly place meat in the pan with the hot oil.

Serves 4

SHOPPING LIST

Veal cutlets, 1 pound (Veal is expensive; you may easily substitute chicken breasts or pork cutlets)

All purpose flour, ½ cup

Salt, ½ teaspoon

Ground pepper, ½ teaspoon

Bread crumbs, ½ cup

Eggs, 2 large

Oil for frying

Lemons, 2

EQUIPMENT

Plastic wrap

Large saute pan

3 shallow bowls

Fry the schnitzel for 3-4 minutes on one side. Turn them over once and fry until both sides are golden brown. Do not crowd the pan, cook the schnitzel in batches. Remove from pan, allow the oil to drain off, place on a plate with lemon wedges.

(see baked apples recipe on page 108)

baked apples stuffed with spicy red cabbage

BRAISED CABBAGE AND APPLES ARE classic components in German cuisine. This is an elegant way of presenting this side dish that will pair perfectly with almost any German entrée.

Preheat the oven to 350° F. Let the butter come to room temperature.

Cut the apple in half horizontally. Shave just enough off the top and bottom of the apples so there is a flat surface and the apple halves are stable enough to stand on end.

Using a knife (or mellon baller), hollow out the apple half, removing the seeds and most of the apple flesh. Leave enough apple flesh to ensure the apple half is structurally sound. The apple halves will look like a small bowl. Evenly spread the butter inside each of the hollowed out apples and sprinkle with cinnamon. Place the apples in the baking dish or muffin pan and place in the oven. Cook for 20 minutes. This step can be done a day in advance.

Remove the core of the cabbage (the tough white part of the cabbage) and thinly slice the cabbage. The slices should be approximately ¼ inches thick. Juice the lemon.

Serves 4

In a medium size pan, heat the olive oil over medium heat. Add the red cabbage, beer, red wine vinegar, red pepper, lemon juice, salt and pepper. Cook over low heat, stirring occasionally, until just tender, about 20 minutes. Check seasoning and add more salt and pepper if needed. This step can be done a day in advance.

Stuff the apples with the cooked cabbage mixture and cook for an additional 10 minutes covered with aluminum foil. If you cook the cabbage and apples in advance, reheat, covered, for 15 minutes or until warmed through.

SHOPPING LIST

Extra-virgin olive oil, ¼ cup

One head of red cabbage, 2 ½ to 3 pounds – cored and sliced ¼ inch thick

Lemon, 1

Red pepper flakes, pinch

Red wine vinegar, ¼ cup

Beer, ¼ cup

Apples, 2 large – golden delicious or Cortland are good varieties to use.

Butter, 2 tablespoons

Cinnamon, 2 teaspoons

EQUIPMENT

Medium sauce pan

Large melon baller (optional)

Small baking dish or muffin tin

apple gingerbread bread pudding

THIS IS A FUN AND unique twist on classic bread pudding. The gingerbread provides an amazing and unexpected depth of flavor to the bread pudding. You can take a shortcut and use a store bought ginger cake; however, it is difficult to find one that will taste as good as a homemade cake.

SHOPPING LIST

All-purpose flour, 1¾ cups

Baking powder, 1 teaspoon

Baking soda, ¾ teaspoon

Salt, ¼ teaspoon

Ground ginger, 2 tablespoons

Crystallized ginger, ⅓ cup (1 ¾ ounces)

Ground cinnamon, 1 teaspoon

Fresh ground nutmeg, ⅓ teaspoon

Butter 4 ounces (1 stick)

Dark brown sugar, ½ cup

Honey, ¼ cup

Eggs, 2 large

Black strap molasses, 6 tablespoons

Whole milk, ¾ cup

EQUIPMENT

9 x 5 inch loaf pan (you can use a disposable pan)

Stand mixer

gingerbread

Makes 1 Loaf

Preheat oven to 350° F. Coat 9 x 5" loaf pan with vegetable spray. Finely chop the crystallized ginger.

In a bowl, combine the flour, baking powder, baking soda, salt, ground ginger, nutmeg and cinnamon, then set aside.

Using a stand mixer, beat the butter and sugar until light and fluffy on medium speed. Beat in the egg and continue beating until combined. Add molasses, crystallized ginger, and milk. Continue beating until everything is incorporated.

Remove the mixing bowl from the stand. Carefully fold in the flour mixture into the butter mixture using a wooden spoon or spatula. Do not mix too aggressively otherwise the gingerbread can become tough. It is fine if there are a few streaks of flour visible.

Pour the batter into the prepared loaf pan. Bake for approximately 50 minutes or until done. Check if the cake is done by sticking a knife or toothpick in the center of the cake. If it comes out clean it is done; if wet batter is sticking it needs more time in the oven. Let the cake cool in the pan.

Makes 8 to 12 servings

Cut the gingerbread into cubes. Remove the core from apple and chop them so the pieces are about the size of an M&M candy. Coat baking dish with non-stick vegetable spray. Add gingerbread pieces and chopped apple to dish and set aside.

In a sauce pan heat the milk and cream. Using a sharp knife, cut the vanilla bean in half lengthwise, scrape the moist seeds in the middle and add the scrapings to the milk and cream mixture. The moist black vanilla scrapings may not look like much but it is pure flavor. Once you begin to smell the vanilla infusing the milk, remove from heat and set aside. Meanwhile, in a bowl, combine the eggs, yolks, sugar, cinnamon, and salt. Hand whip until mixed.

Make sure the milk and cream mixture has cooled to room temperature. Add the egg mixture and mix thoroughly. Pour the liquid mixture over the cubed gingerbread. Press the gingerbread down to ensure the cake soaks up the liquid. Let sit for one hour or overnight. I prefer the overnight soak as it allows the cake to really absorb the liquid and results in a better end product.

Preheat oven to 350° F.

Cover the pan with foil and bake for approximately 1 hour or until done. Remove the foil during the last 20 minutes of baking to brown the top. You can tell if it is done when the center just starts to become firm and the bread pudding doubles in height. Baking times may vary with your oven. Cut into squares and serve warm with whipped cream or vanilla ice cream.

SHOPPING LIST

Gingerbread cake, 1 loaf (see gingerbread recipe left page)

Apple, 1 large (Jonagold, Braeburn, Golden Delicious, or Gala varieties are good choices)

Whole milk, 2 cups

Cream, ¾ cup

Whole vanilla bean, 1 (can substitute 2 teaspoons of vanilla extract)

Eggs, 3 large whole

Egg yolks, 2

Sugar, ½ cup

Cinnamon, ½ teaspoon

EQUIPMENT

8 x 8 inch baking dish

Sauce pan

Mixing bowl

culinary notes

culinary notes

COOKING WITH KIDDOS

... Dinosaur eggs

... Super crunchy fish sticks

... Mac 'n cheese

... Violet's chocolate pudding

JUST AS COOKING WITH A romantic interest is a great bonding experience, the same holds true for when you cook with children.

Five reasons why you should cook with kids, not just for them.

- It is fun!!

- Kids will be more inclined to eat what they make. Maybe it is taking pride in what they help create, but they will be more likely to eat whatever they had a hand in making.

- Practice creativity and imagination. Kids find cooking activities enjoyable because they are able to create.

- They are working together as a team, whether it is with a parent or with a sibling to get the job done.

- It is a fun way to carve out family time and bonding.

Take time to cook with your kids and they will have memories that they, in turn, can pass on to their families. It may take a longer time to get the meal or snack done but the moments with your children will be priceless. Keep things in perspective and do not stress about the flour on the floor or spilled milk.

dinosaur eggs

KIDS LIKE COLORFUL DISHES AND they will love this one. It makes a great after-school snack.

SHOPPING LIST

Eggs, 4

Carrot stick, 1

Low fat mayonnaise, ⅓ cup

Frozen peas, ¼ cup

Iceberg lettuce, 4 large leaves

EQUIPMENT

Small sauce pan with a lid

Vegetable peeler

Makes 4 servings

Defrost the peas.

Hard boil the eggs. Place 4 eggs in a saucepan and add enough cold tap water to completely cover the eggs by 1 inch. Bring to a rolling boil over high heat. Once the water is boiling, turn off the heat and leave covered for 10 minutes. After 10 minutes place eggs under ice cold water or in a bowl of ice and water to chill. Leave them for a few minutes in the cold water until the egg is completely cooled. This step keeps the yolk bright yellow and prevents a greenish "ring" from forming on the surface of the yolk. Peel the shell from the eggs and set the eggs aside.

Cut the eggs in half lengthwise and remove the yolks. In a small bowl mix the 4 yolks, mayonnaise and peas. Salt and pepper to taste. Carefully spoon the egg mixture back into the egg white halves.

Using the vegetable peeler, peel at least eight long ribbons of carrot. On each lettuce leaf, place a few carrot ribbons and place an egg half on top.

Encourage the kids to eat it like a lettuce wrap.

super crunchy fish sticks

THIS VERSION IS SO MUCH healthier than the highly processed fish sticks you find in the freezer section of supermarkets.

Makes 4 servings

Preheat oven to 450° F.

Place Grape-Nuts cereal, cereal flakes, and a healthy pinch of salt in a food processor and process until finely ground. Transfer to a shallow dish.

Cut the fish into ½ inch strips.

Place flour in a second shallow dish and beaten eggs in a third shallow dish. Dredge each strip of fish in the flour, dip it in the egg and then coat all sides with the breadcrumb mixture. Place on the prepared baking sheet. Coat the breaded fish generously with cooking spray.

Bake until the fish is cooked through and the breading is a rich golden brown and crisp, about 10 minutes.

Let cool for a few minutes and serve with tartar sauce.

SHOPPING LIST

Canola oil cooking spray

Grape-Nuts Cereal, 1 cup

Whole-grain cereal flakes, 1 cup

All-purpose flour, ½ cup

Eggs, 2 large

Tilapia fillets, 1 pound (Substitute any firm white flesh fish like Halibut or Orange Roughy)

Your favorite prepared tartar sauce for dipping

EQUIPMENT

Baking sheet with non-stick silicone pad

Vegetable spray

Food processor

3 shallow dishes

mac 'n cheese

EVERY KID (even the middle-aged ones) will love this dish. It is easy and quick to make on the stove top.

In a large pot of boiling salted water cook the pasta to al dente and drain. The pasta should still have a little "bite" to it since it will continue to cook when mixed with the cheese. Return to the pot and melt in the butter. Toss to coat.

Whisk together in a small bowl the eggs, evaporated milk, salt, pepper, and mustard. Stir this mixture into the pasta and add the cheese. Reduce the heat to low, and continue to stir for 3 minutes or until creamy.

Makes 4 servings

SHOPPING LIST

Elbow macaroni, ½ pound

Butter, 4 tablespoons

Eggs, 2

Evaporated milk, 6 ounces

Dijon mustard, ½ teaspoon

Sharp cheddar, 10 ounces shredded

EQUIPMENT

4 quart pot (or larger)

Strainer for pasta

Small mixing bowl

violet's chocolate pudding

"This chocolate pudding is a million times better than pudding cups."
—Violet, 5 years old

THIS IS A FUN RECIPE to make with kids. While it may be tempting to buy the instant version sold in the little boxes, the difference with this recipe is the quality of the chocolate. After your first spoonful, this recipe will instantly become one of your all time favorites.

In a heavy-bottom medium-sized saucepan, whisk together sugar, cocoa powder, corn starch and a pinch of salt. Add a ½ cup of cream, all of the milk and 4 egg yolks. Whisk until thoroughly combined.

Stir in chocolate chips and set pan over medium-low heat. Whisk slowly and constantly, making sure to scrape sides of pan, just until pudding begins to boil, about 7 to 8 minutes. It is important to constantly stir the pudding mixture so it will have a smooth final consistency. The pudding will continue to thicken as it cools, and more so once it is refrigerated.

Remove saucepan from heat and transfer pudding mixture to a medium bowl. Stir in vanilla. Cover with plastic and refrigerate until thick and well chilled, approximately 4 hours or overnight.

When you are ready to serve, make the whip cream. Beat together 1 cup heavy cream and confectioners' sugar to form soft peaks. Top pudding with whipped cream.

Makes 4 large servings

SHOPPING LIST

Vanilla extract, 2 teaspoons

Whole milk, 1 ½ cups

Heavy cream, 1 ½ cups

Sugar, 6 tablespoons

Corn starch, 4 tablespoons

Cocoa powder, 1 tablespoon unsweetened

Bittersweet chocolate, 9 ounces (60-70% cocoa)

Egg, 4 yolks

Confectioners' sugar, 1 tablespoon (it is sometimes called powdered sugar)

EQUIPMENT

Medium-size saucepan

Whisk

Mixing bowls, medium & large

Rubber spatula

Mixing spoon

DOUBLE DATE NIGHT
10

... Brie en croute and spinach salad

... Olive oil poached halibut with mint pesto

... Fennel and spinach strudel

... Pomegranate semifreddo with chocolate sauce

IT IS SOMETIMES MORE ENJOYABLE to entertain a couple in the comfort of your own home than it is to head out to a restaurant.

Make the dinner interactive by having your friends help with preparing and serving dinner. Guests gravitate to the kitchen anyway and then find themselves doing a little dance to avoid getting in the way. Assigning everybody tasks gets them engaged in the dinner and keeps things fun. It also helps guests feel more than just invited, but also needed.

Give tasks that are straightforward and fun. Avoid the temptation to pass off tasks that you do not enjoy. Even my closest friends will head for the door if I ask them to start peeling the beets.

brie en croute and spinach salad

I LIKE SALADS ONLY IF they are interesting, and this salad is very interesting. If strawberries or blueberries are in season, you can substitute fresh fruit instead of dried fruit. The brie en croute acts as both croutons and cheese for the salad. Check with your date and other guests if they are lactose intolerant otherwise things could get ugly.

Preheat oven to 350° F.

Put pecans in a shallow pan in the oven for 5-10 minutes. The nuts will become fragrant and slightly brown. Remove and set aside.

Raise oven to 375° F. Beat egg yolk with 1 tablespoon water for an egg wash, set aside.

Thaw puff pastry for 20 minutes, then unfold and smooth out any seams.

Carefully cut the brie in half across the middle so you end up with two circles. WIth one half of the cheese rind side down, spoon the jam in the middle of the brie. Cover with the other half of the brie so you have reassembled the original shape of brie. You have just made a brie and jam sandwich. Place Brie on half of the puff pastry and fold over the pastry to completely cover the cheese. The puff pastry should have a ½ inch border larger than the brie and cut away extra pastry dough. Brush border with egg mixture and press tightly to seal the edges.

Makes 4 servings

SHOPPING LIST

Egg, 1 yolk only

Frozen puff pastry, 1 sheet

Brie, 1 small wheel approximately 3 ounces

Apricot jam, 1 ½ tablespoons (can substitute any fruit jam that is not too sweet)

Spinach, 4 ounces (about 6 cups)

Dried blueberries, ½ cup (can substitute raisins)

Raw pecans pieces, ½ cup unsalted

Lemons, 2 for juice

Olive oil, ½ cup

EQUIPMENT

Large mixing bowl

Baking sheet

Silicone non-stick pad

Make a small slot in the top of the pastry to allow steam to vent. This can all be done earlier in the day, and all of the above steps can be done in advance and stored in the refrigerator.

Brush top only with egg wash and on lined sheet pan in the middle of a preheated 375° F oven. Bake for 20 minutes or until the puff pastry is golden brown.

Let cool 10 minutes.

spinach salad

In a large mixing bowl add the juice of 2 lemons, olive oil and salt and pepper to taste. Add the spinach and using your clean hands, gently mix so the spinach becomes lightly but evenly coated. Divide the spinach between 4 plates and evenly divide the pecans and dried blueberries. Cut the brie into 4 pieces and place on top of the spinach salad

olive oil poached halibut with mint lemon pesto

AT SOME POINT IN ANY relationship you will find yourself entertaining another couple. Embrace it. What I like about this fish preparation is that it is done in the oven and will not leave your kitchen smelling like a fish-and-chips shop. Halibut is a mild, lean fish that most everyone enjoys. Pacific halibut is an environmentally safe choice. The fish will come out moist and flaky, but pale in color. Pairing it with a mint pesto adds splashes of both color and bright flavor.

mint pesto

In a food processor, combine ½ the bunch of mint leaves with ¼ the bunch of parsley leaves, 2 garlic cloves, juice from 2 lemons and zest of 1 lemon. Pulse until finely chopped. With the machine running, drizzle 2 tablespoons of olive oil in a thin stream and process until smooth. You can add more olive oil to get the consistency you want. Season the pesto with salt and pepper. You can make the pesto a day ahead.

Makes 4 servings

halibut

Preheat oven to 200° F.

Take the fish out of the refrigerator 30 minutes before you plan on cooking and season it with salt and pepper. Don't worry, the fish will not spoil. By allowing it come to room temperature, it will help the fish cook evenly.

In a skillet that is large enough to hold the fish in a single layer without overcrowding, heat the olive oil over medium low heat. Slice a lemon into thin slices and roughly chop 2 garlic cloves. The oil should begin to simmer very slightly and you will see occasional bubbles rising to the surface. Gently place the fish in the oil, making sure the fish is completely covered in oil. Add the lemon slices and chopped garlic cloves and place the skillet in the oven.

Poach until a few small whitish droplets rise to the surface of the fish and the fish maintains a trace of transparency in the middle, 25-35 minutes. Transfer the halibut to a plate so it can drain for a few minutes. Serve with a healthy dollop of mint pesto over the fish.

SHOPPING LIST

Olive oil, 4 ½ cups

Garlic, 4 cloves

Halibut, 4 (6-ounce) pieces with the skin and bones removed (Can substitute red snapper or cod)

Lemons, 3

Packed fresh mint leaves, 1 bunch

Flat-leaf parsley, 1 bunch

EQUIPMENT

10-inch skillet pan

Food processor

Lemon zester

fennel and spinach strudel

THIS IS A NEAR PERFECT side dish for the olive oil poached halibut. It has amazing flavor, great texture and vibrant color. It can be made a day ahead and warmed up at the same time you are poaching the fish. The only tricky part is working with phyllo dough if you have not played with this kind of dough before.

In a saucepan cook the spinach according to the package instructions, drain it, and let it cool. When the spinach is cool enough to handle, squeeze it dry by handfuls, transferring it as it is squeezed to a bowl. Don't be afraid to get your hands dirty; you want the spinach very dry. Mince the shallot and chop only the white bulb of the fennel into small pieces. You chop the fennel bulb the same way you would chop an onion. In a saucepan cook the shallot, nutmeg powder, fennel seeds and chopped fennel bulb in 2 tablespoons of butter over moderate heat, stirring until the vegetables are softened. Stir in the flour and cook the mixture for another minute. Add the anise flavored spirit and cook the mixture for 3 minutes, stirring constantly. The mixture should be very thick; you do not want a dripping strudel. Stir the fennel mixture into the spinach with the Parmesan and salt and pepper to taste. The filling may be made 1 day in advance and stored in the refrigerator.

Preheat the oven to 425°F. Defrost the phyllo dough according to the directions on the package. Cover the phyllo dough with the damp kitchen towel so the dough does not dry out.

Makes 4 servings

In a small saucepan or in a glass bowl in the microwave, melt the remaining butter. Have a damp kitchen towel handy. Put 1 sheet of the phyllo on the wax paper, brush it with some of the butter. Place the damp cloth over the other phyllo sheets so they do not dry out while you are assembling the strudel. You will assemble a stack of 6 sheets of phyllo dough, brushing melted butter between each layer sheet of phyllo dough. Think of it as a phyllo dough and butter lasagna. The dough is very thin and fragile so work slowly. Do not worry if a sheet tears, you can still add it to the layered sheets, just brush it with a little extra butter. Pastry brushes are the easiest way to spread the butter, but you can also use a clean finger or a paper towel.

Spread about ⅔ of the spinach filling in a 3-inch-wide strip, mounding it on the phyllo 4 inches above the nearest long side, leaving a 2-inch border at each end. Carefully lift the bottom 4 inches of the pastry over the filling, fold in the ends, and roll up the strudel tightly. It should be a tightly rolled log (and look like a very big burrito). Transfer the strudel carefully, seam side down, to the lined baking sheet, brush the top with the remaining butter, and bake it in the lower third of the oven for 25 minutes, or until it is golden brown. Let the strudel cool to warm on the baking sheet on a rack.

The strudel may be made 1 day in advance and kept covered loosely in the refrigerator. To reheat, put into the oven the same time you put the olive oil poached halibut in the oven and it will be warmed through the same time the halibut is cooked. Cut into 4 thick slices.

The leftover spinach/fennel mixture makes an amazing omelet stuffing the next morning.

SHOPPING LIST

Frozen chopped spinach, two 10-ounce packages

Shallot, 1 each

Fennel bulb, 1 small (sometimes called anise)

Fennel seed, 2 teaspoons

Ground nutmeg, ½ teaspoon

Butter, 1 stick (½ cup)

All-purpose or whole wheat flour, 2 tablespoons

Ouzo or Richard, or other anise-flavored spirit, 2 tablespoons

Grated Parmesan, 4 ounces

One box of frozen phyllo sheets, you will need 6-8 sheets

EQUIPMENT

Sauce pan

Damp kitchen towel

Baking sheet

Non-stick silicone pad

pomegranate semifreddo with chocolate sauce

SEMIFREDDO MEANS SEMI-FROZEN IN ITALIAN. It is a dessert that is similar to ice cream but does not require any special equipment. What I love about this dish is that you make the dessert in advance with very little effort yet still dazzle your guests.

In a medium stainless-steel bowl, whisk the eggs with the sugar and pomegranate liqueur. Set the bowl over a large saucepan of simmering water and whisk constantly until the mixture turns bright yellow and thickens, about 10 minutes. Be careful not let the eggs get too hot or they will scramble. Remove the bowl from the heat and continue whisking for a few minutes. Set aside and let cool to room temperature. Roughly chop the pistachio nuts and fold into the egg mixture.

In a large bowl, beat the cream to soft peaks with the whisk or immersion blender. Fold the cream into the egg mixture. Spoon the semifreddo into an airtight container, cover with plastic wrap and freeze until firm, at least 6 hours or up to 5 days.

Prior to serving, remove the semifreddo from the freezer and let stand at room temperature for 5 to 10 minutes so it will soften slightly.

At the same time, melt the chocolate over low heat in a small saucepan, stirring occasionally. Scoop the semifreddo into 4 large wine glasses; drizzle with the melted chocolate.

Makes 4 servings

SHOPPING LIST

Eggs, 2 large

Sugar, ½ cup

Pomegranate liqueur, 2 tablespoons

Shelled and salted pistachio nuts, 6 ounces

Heavy cream, 1 cup

Bittersweet chocolate chips, 3 ounces

EQUIPMENT

Stainless steel bowl

Sauce pan

Large mixing bowl

Whisk or immersion blender

Plastic container with a tight fitting lid, 5 cups or larger

4 large wine glasses

ice cream scoop

culinary notes

culinary notes

ROMANTIC DINNER (SPRING/SUMMER)

... Beet grapefruit salad

... Chicken piperade over wasabi cauliflower puree

... Haricot Verts with tarragon butter and black sesame seeds

... White chocolate ginger mousse

FEW THINGS ARE MORE PERSONAL or intimate than cooking dinner for a romantic interest. You do not have to spend a lot of money on crystal glasses and fine china, but you do want to set the right mood. When planning the menu for a romantic dinner during the spring or summer season, it should reflect what is seasonal at the market. Lighter dishes and greater use of vegetables is what your guest expects to see.

CANDLES

Lighting a few unscented candles will do wonders. A gentleman does not own scented candles. Seriously.

MUSIC

Soft background music is supposed to be just that, keep the volume low. It is hard to go wrong with classics like jazz, blues or Barry White. Avoid the cliché love songs; most are just cheesy. If you can add a few of her favorite songs into the playlist you will score serious bonus points.

LOCATION

Dinner does not have to be served only in the dining room! If your kitchen has a counter, serve dinner on the counter and use cooking as entertainment. If there is a romantic movie that she has dropped hints she wants to see, rent the DVD and serve dinner in front of the television like an indoor picnic.

beet grapefruit salad

IF YOU HAVE BEEN RELUCTANT to cook with beets before, get over it because they are delicious. This dish strikes an amazing balance amongst the sweet earthiness of the beets, acidity of the grapefruit and creaminess of the blue cheese and avocado. Trust me, women find men who eat beets desirable.

Preheat oven to 400° F. Trim the greens off the beets if they have them and wrap the beets in foil. Roast until beets are tender when pierced with fork, about 1 hour. Cool beets to room temperature. (Can be prepared 1 day ahead. Refrigerate beets in their foil packets.)

When the beets are cool enough to handle, open the aluminum foil packets over a bowl or plate to catch any liquid that may come out. Using a paper towel, rub the beets to slip off the skins. They will come off easily. Cut beets into ¾-inch pieces and set aside.

The only tricky part of this recipe is removing the peel, pith and membrane from the grapefruit so you are left with just the flesh. Trim both ends of grapefruit so that you see the flesh and it sits (but does not wobble) on the cutting board. Starting at the top of the grapefruit, trim the skin and white pith off, following the curvature of the fruit. You do not want to cut too much fruit away, but definitely remove all of the white pith. Repeat along all sides until the skin is removed and all you see is the flesh. Holding the grapefruit over a bowl, you will see the flesh segments separated by thin membranes. Cut along one membrane and then push up the other side of the segment so that the grapefruit segment comes out cleanly with no membrane. Keep working around the grapefruit so that all of the grapefruit is removed. Over the same bowl squeeze the membrane to capture any remaining juice.

Set aside 2 tablespoons of the grapefruit juice to make the dressing. Set aside the grapefruit segments. If you mangle the grapefruit segments, don't worry. It may not look as pretty but the salad will still be delicious.

Makes 2 large servings

SHOPPING LIST

Beets, 2 medium

Grapefruits, 2 medium (they can be pink or red grapefruits)

Sherry wine vinegar, 1 ½ tablespoons

Dijon mustard, 1 teaspoon

Extra-virgin olive oil, ½ cup

Pre-washed mixed baby greens, a 5-ounce bag

Avocado, 1 medium size and ripe

Blue cheese, 1 ounce

EQUIPMENT

Mixing bowl

Aluminum foil

dressing

To make the dressing, whisk together the vinegar, mustard and 2 tablespoons of reserved grapefruit juice in small bowl to blend. Gradually whisk in oil. Season to taste with salt and pepper.

assembly

Cut the avocado in half lengthwise and twist apart. Carefully slice the side that has the large pit in half and use a knife to remove the pit. Using a large spoon, go underneath the skin and scoop out the flesh on both sides. If the avocado is ripe, it will come out easily. Cut the avocado into ½ inch pieces.

Toss greens and ¾ cup of the dressing in large bowl. Season to taste with salt and pepper. Divide salad among 10 plates. Scatter beets, grapefruit, avocados, and crumbled blue cheese over salads, dividing equally. Drizzle with remaining dressing.

chicken piperade over wasabi cauliflower puree

THIS COLORFUL DISH IS A twist on a classic dish from the Basque region of Spain. It can easily be prepared in advance and looks gorgeous when served. The cauliflower puree is a tasty, low fat alternative to mashed potatoes. Your female dinner guest will appreciate you looking out for her and not just looking at her figure.

Cut the chicken crosswise into 1 inch strips. Put 2 tablespoons of the sherry vinegar in bowl. Put the chicken on top of the vinegar, turning it to coat, and allow the chicken to marinate for about 15 minutes at room temperature.

Cut the florets off the cauliflower and discard the tough core. Boil cauliflower florets in water until very tender, about 20 minutes. Drain and place in a food processor, add olive oil and sour cream, one tablespoon at a time until a smooth consistency--similar to mashed potatoes, is reached. Season to taste with wasabi and salt and pepper. This can be prepared in advance and reheated in the microwave.

Melt butter in a large skillet over medium high heat. Pat the chicken dry and season it well with salt and pepper. Brown the chicken well. Don't be afraid to let the chicken pick up color! It adds a lot of flavor to the dish even though the chicken will be not be fully cooked-through. The chicken will finish cooking in the final steps of the recipe. Thinly slice the onion.

Makes 4 servings

SHOPPING LIST

Sherry vinegar, 3 tablespoons

Skinless chicken breasts, ¾ pound boneless

Butter, 2 tablespoons

Onion, 1 small

Red bell peppers, 1

Garlic cloves, 3

Cayenne pepper, ¼ teaspoon

Cherry tomatoes, 4

Ham, 2 ounces

Watercress, 1 cup (Can substitute spinach) roughly chopped

Cauliflower, 1 medium head

Extra virgin olive oil, 2 to 3 tablespoons

Light sour cream, 4 tablespoons

Wasabi paste, 1 to 2 teaspoons, to taste

EQUIPMENT

Large pot to boil cauliflower

Food processor

Large skillet

Remove the chicken from the pan and keep warm on a plate. Add the onions to the pan and lower the heat to medium-low. Allow the onions to cook slowly for about 15 minutes, stirring occasionally. Remove the seeds from the red pepper and slice into thin strips. Mince the garlic, cut the ham into thin strips and cut the tomatoes in half. Add the red bell peppers, garlic and cayenne powder to the onions and cook until the peppers are very tender, about 15 to 20 minutes. Add the chicken, tomatoes, ham and remaining tablespoon of sherry vinegar.

Cover and continue cooking until the chicken is cooked completely, about 5 to 7 minutes. There should be a very flavorful juice in the pan. Chop up the watercress and add it to the dish, it should almost melt into the sauce. Stir to combine. Serve over the wasabi cauliflower puree.

haricot verts with tarragon butter and black sesame seeds

HARICOTS VERTS ARE ALSO SOMETIME called green beans. Their slender, elegant shape and bright green color are a great addition to any plate. Combined with black sesame seeds, it is one of the sexier side dishes you can make.

Makes 2 servings

SHOPPING LIST

- Butter, 1 ½ tablespoons
- Shallot, 1 small
- Tarragon, 5-6 stalks
- Fresh lemon juice, 1 teaspoon
- Haricots verts, ½ lb preferably fresh, but frozen work fine
- Black sesame seeds, 1 ounce

EQUIPMENT

- Sauté pan
- Microwave

Rinse the haricot verts but do not dry them. Place them on a plate with what water is clinging to the beans and microwave for a minute. They should begin to soften and be slightly tender. If they are still firm, microwave for an additional 30 seconds.

Finely chop the tarragon leaves. In a sauté pan over medium heat melt the butter and add the shallots. Cook for 3-5 minutes until the shallots are soft and translucent, add the chopped tarragon leaves. Add the beans and cook for another 5 minutes, season to taste with salt and pepper. This can be done in advance and re-heated before serving.

Divide between two plates and generously sprinkle the black sesame seeds over the beans.

white chocolate ginger mousse

THE SHORT SHOPPING LIST BETRAYS the elegance and depth of flavor of this dessert. This sensual dessert is sweet and slightly spicy and can easily be made a day or two in advance. Ginger is also a rumored aphrodisiac. This dish was inspired by trying to impress a friend after she mentioned her love for whipped desserts and white chocolate … and it worked.

Makes 2 servings

In a small sauce pan, over low heat, melt the white chocolate along with 4 tablespoons of cream, ginger powder and corn syrup until the mixture is smooth. Remove from heat and cool until barely lukewarm.

Using stand mixer or immersion blender, beat ¾ cup cream and confectioners' sugar in medium bowl to medium-firm peaks (it will look and taste like whiped cream). Carefully fold cream into white chocolate mixture. You want to be gentle with the whiped cream when you fold in the chocolate ginger mixture otherwise the final product will not be light and fluffy. Cover and refrigerate until firm, about 4 hours. (Can be prepared 2 days ahead.)

To serve, place the mousse into a sealable, disposable plastic bag. Snip off a corner of the bag and pipe into wine glasses. Garnish with fresh seasonal berries and chocolate shavings.

SHOPPING LIST

White chocolate, 4 ounces chopped (use a high quality one such as Lindt)

Heavy cream, 5 ounces (a total of 11 tablespoons)

Light corn syrup, 1 tablespoon

Ground ginger, 2 teaspoons

Confectioners' sugar, ¼ cup

Berries for garnish, ½ cup (if available and in season, raspberries and blackberries)

Dark chocolate for shavings as garnish (optional)

EQUIPMENT

Small sauce pan

Stand mixer or immersion blender

Wine glasses

culinary notes

culinary notes

Romantic Dinner (Spring/Summer)

12 ROMANTIC DINNER ANOTHER NIGHT (FALL/WINTER)

... Farmers market grilled chopped salad with blood orange vinaigrette

... Syrah braised and grilled short ribs on a bed of mascarpone/jalapeño polenta

... Pomegranate glazed carrots

... Poached pears with dark chocolate sauce

THE IDEA OF A ROMANTIC dinner in the fall or winter creates the mental image of sitting with your romantic interest in front of a roaring fireplace. Most of us do not have a fireplace and have to be more creative to set the right intimate setting. A gentleman can use conversation to set the mood.

PAY ATTENTION TO HER

Let's be serious, women love attention. No matter who she is, where she is or what she does, women do enjoy you paying attention to them. This is especially true when it comes to her romantic relationships. Every woman is different in the amount of attention she may need or want. However, as you get to know one another, you will learn different things about each other. When she reveals her favorites, acknowledge and recognize them as clues for how to romance her.

REMEMBER AND ACKNOWLEDGE HER PREFERENCES

Acknowledge and remember her likes and dislikes, regardless of what they may be. The personal preferences and dislikes of any particular woman will clue you in on how to romance her. The things that you recognize as her favorites will also come in quite handy while shopping for special occasions, holidays and every other day.

BE GENUINE

Women seem to have an intuitive bullshit detector. Do not try to be someone else, just be yourself. If she was not interested in being with you, then you wouldn't be cooking dinner for her.

TAKE THOUGHTFUL ACTION

Now that you are paying attention to her and acknowledging her favorites, you need to take the time to consider how to take action for romance. Above and beyond everything else, you should always be true to yourself. Learning how to romance a woman involves being yourself and doing those things that you discover as clues for winning her heart.

farmers market grilled chopped salad with blood orange vinaigrette

WHILE THE SPECIFIC VEGETABLES AVAILABLE will vary by location, the underlying goal is to focus on seasonal products. Almost every city now has a farmers market and by buying your produce there you will be steered toward items at the peak of flavor. Your romantic interest will be impressed that you care about her to serve a healthy salad. You can even invite her to join you at the farmers market for a fun morning together. Do not hesitate to substitute other fresh vegetables; just maintain a balance of flavor, color and texture in the salad. I always include brussel sprouts while they are in season because an incredibly beautiful friend who happens to be a vegetarian loves her brussel sprouts.

vinaigrette

Make the vinaigrette up to 2 days in advance. Mince the shallot and mince the tarragon leaves throwing out the stems. Mix the shallots, tarragon leaves, and mustard. Slowly drizzle in the olive oil while whisking briskly. The salad dressing will come together; the mustard helps the oil and vinegar stay together. Refrigerate until ready to use.

Makes 2 servings

If you have a barbeque, grill the vegetables outside. If you do not have a grill or it is too cold to cook outside you use the broiler. Preheat the grill or broiler.

Peel the parsnip. Cut off the stalk of the broccoli, you will be left with just the head of florets. On a baking sheet, put the peeled parsnip, broccoli, Brussels sprouts and radicchio half. Using a pastry brush, paper towel or your fingers, brush the vegetables with the vegetable oil. Season all the vegetables liberally with salt. Broil until the vegetables start to brown, 8-12 minutes. Remove from the oven and let cool until you can handle them. Chop all the vegetables into small pieces; cut the Brussels sprouts into quarters and try to cut all of the other vegetables to match that size.

In a mixing bowl combine the chopped vegetables and half the dressing. Make sure all of the vegetables are coated with dressing, but there should not be a pool of dressing at the bottom of the bowl. Add additional dressing as necessary. Divide the salad between two plates, add crumbled feta cheese and serve.

SHOPPING LIST

Broccoli, ½ head

Brussels sprouts, 1 pint

Parsnips, 1 medium

Radicchio, ½ of one head
  (it looks like a small head of red lettuce)

Vegetable oil, 2 tablespoons

Coarse grain mustard,
  1 rounded teaspoon

Blood Orange vinegar,
  2 tablespoons (Can substitute sherry vinegar)

Extra-virgin olive oil,
  5 tablespoons

Tarragon (optional) 3 sprigs

Shallot, 1 medium

Feta cheese, 1 ounce

EQUIPMENT

Mixing bowl

Baking sheet

syrah braised and grilled short ribs on a bed of mascarpone jalapeño polenta

I CONSIDER THIS DISH ROMANTIC comfort food. Imagine the luscious meat sitting on a bed of creamy polenta that has a subtle bite from the jalapeño. Most of the preparation can be done the day before, giving you time to charm her and not spend the entire evening in the kitchen.

DO AHEAD

Preheat the oven to 325° F.

Season the ribs with salt and pepper.

In a large skillet, heat the vegetable oil. Roughly chop the bacon and cook it over medium heat until crisp, 6-8 minutes. Using a slotted spoon, remove the bacon and set aside but leave the rendered bacon fat in the pan.

Working in two batches, add the ribs to the skillet and cook over moderately high heat, turning a few times, until richly browned and crusty on all sides, about 8 - 10 minutes per batch. You work in two batches to ensure that the pan is not overcrowded which would not allow the meat to brown enough. Remove the ribs and set aside.

Roughly chop the shallot, mushrooms, garlic and carrot. Add them to the sauté pan and cook over moderately high heat, stirring occasionally, until lightly browned, about 5 minutes. Add the bacon, bay leaf and beef ribs back to the pan and pour the wine and beef broth over the ribs. The liquid should cover at least half of the meat, but not drown them entirely.

Cover and braise in the oven for about 4 hours, turning the ribs once, until the meat is very tender and almost falling off the bone.

Remove from heat and let cool in braising liquid. If you do not let the meat cool in the braising liquid then the meat will become dry. Use the slotted spoon to remove the vegetables and bacon pieces and discard, they have given all they can and will not have any flavor left. Do all of this night before or even 2 days in advance and refrigerate the ribs in the braising liquid.

Makes 2 servings

SHOPPING LIST

Short ribs on the bone, 4 thick meaty pieces (2-2.5 pounds)

Bay leaf, 1

Fresh thyme, 2 sprigs

Vegetable oil, 1 tablespoon

Bacon, ¼ pound

Shallot, 1

Carrot, 1

Garlic, 2 cloves

mushrooms, 4 ounces

Syrah or other dry red wine, ¾ cups

Beef broth, ½ cup

Low sodium chicken stock, 32 ounces

Butter, 4 ounces (1 stick)

Yellow polenta, 9 ounces (250 grams)

Mascarpone cheese, 3 ounces

Jalapeño, 1 small

EQUIPMENT

Large heavy sauce pan with a lid or a casserole dish that you can use on the cook top

Sauce pan

Grill pan (optional)

THE NIGHT OF THE DINNER

Take the short ribs out the refrigerator. When the ribs and sauce are refrigerated, fat in the sauce will rise to the surface and harden, turning white. Using a fork, skim off the fat and throw away. Let the ribs and sauce come to room temperature.

Make the polenta. In a sauce pan, boil 16 ounces of water, chicken stock and add the butter. Slowly pour the polenta into the hot liquid, whisking briskly to prevent clumping. Reduce the heat to low and cook, whisking constantly, for about 10 minutes, or until the liquid is absorbed. While the polenta is cooking, cut the jalapeño in half, remove the seeds and finely mince. Turn off the heat and add the mascarpone and minced jalapeño peppers. It will stay hot for around 20 minutes. You can also do this in advance and gently reheat in the microwave when ready to serve.

Pour the braising liquid into a sauce pan and heat over medium high heat. Bring to a boil and boil until the liquid reduces by half. At the same time, heat a grill pan over high heat. If you do not have a grill pan, you can use a sauté pan. Cook the short ribs for a few minutes, until they get crusty on all sides.

To serve, place a heaping mound of polenta on the plate and place 2 ribs on top of the polenta. Spoon some of the sauce over the ribs.

pomegranate glazed carrots

THE NATURAL SWEETNESS OF CARROTS combined with the rich mahogany color and flavor of the pomegranate glaze makes this side dish a winner.

SHOPPING LIST

Butter, 1 teaspoon

Carrots, ½ pound

Pomegranate juice, ½ cup

Cinnamon stick, 1 (or 1 teaspoon of powder)

Lemon, 1 small for zest

EQUIPMENT

Zester

Sauté pan

Makes 2 servings

Peel the carrots and cut into diagonal slices around ¼ inch thick.

Heat the butter in a large saute pan over moderate heat. Add carrots and sauté, stirring occasionally for 5 minutes. Add pomegranate juice and cinnamon stick and simmer, stirring occasionally. Cook until carrots are tender and liquid is reduced to a glaze, 20 to 25 minutes. Add the zest from the lemon and salt and pepper to taste. Discard cinnamon stick and serve carrots hot or at room temperature.

poached pears with dark chocolate sauce

THE ELEGANT DESSERT IS SO easy to make. The silky texture of poached pears combined with the aphrodisiac qualities of chocolate makes this dessert a winner.

Makes 2 servings

SHOPPING LIST

Pears, 2 small firm-ripe (preferably Bosc)

White wine, 1 cup (Riesling or Viognier)

Sugar, ¼ cup

Cinnamon stick, 1 broken in half

Bittersweet or semisweet chocolate, 4 ounces

EQUIPMENT

small sauce pan

melon baller, optional but it helps

In a saucepan just large enough to hold pears upright in one layer, bring to a simmer 1 cup of water, white wine, sugar, cinnamon stick, 10 minutes to blend flavors and dissolve the sugar.

Cut a thin slice from bottom of each pear so they will stand upright. Core pears to remove the seeds from the bottom of the pears with a melon baller or small knife and peel the pears, leaving stems intact.

Add pears to poaching liquid and simmer until tender when pierced with a sharp knife and pears become opaque in color, 15 to 20 minutes.

Remove the cinnamon stick and discard. Remove the pears and set aside. Bring the poaching liquid to a boil and boil the liquid until reduced by half. Add chocolate and whisk until chocolate melts and sauce is smooth.

You can poach the pears and make the sauce up to 2 days in advance. Cover and store pears and chocolate sauce separately and refrigerate. To serve, let the pears come to room temperature and warm the sauce.

Serve in a flat bowl with the pear on a thin bed of chocolate sauce and more chocolate sauce drizzled on top.

Romantic Dinner Another Night (Fall/Winter)

culinary notes

culinary notes

13 BREAKFAST IN BED

... Brioche French Toast stuffed with Strawberries and cream

... Ginger scones with peach bellini jam

... Low fat granola parfait

SERVING SOMEONE BREAKFAST IN BED is the most intimate thing you can do in the bedroom … that involves utensils and a coffee mug.

You cannot have a good breakfast without good coffee. The aroma alone of freshly brewed coffee will set the mood. This is the time to experiment with coffee from different regions. Buy your coffee from a coffee shop or supermarket where you can have it ground when you buy it to ensure freshness.

My preference is to use a French press to make coffee, but almost any coffee maker can make a good cup.

ARABIA & AFRICA: Includes coffees from Kenya, Tanzania, Zimbabwe and Ethiopia.

- Ethiopian coffee: This is a complex coffee with light spicy tones and a fruity flavor that some people compare to the taste of dry red wine. As the "birthplace of coffee," Ethiopia has a unique place in the coffee world.

- Kenyan coffee: The coffee is known for its very acidic taste you taste right away in the mouth, and then followed by a medium body with an aftertaste of earthy flavor.

- Tanzania Peaberry: This is a bright and rich coffee, medium body with a delicate acidity, and some hints of wine.

THE AMERICAS: Includes coffees from Colombia, Costa Rica And Guatemala.

- Colombian coffee: Colombian Arabica coffee is perhaps the most well-known, mostly due to our friend Juan Valdez and his mule Conchita. Their coffee is known for the rich flavor and balanced taste.

- Costa Rican coffee: Costa Rican coffees are balanced, clean, with bright acidity featuring citrus or berry-like flavors and hints of chocolate and spice in the finish.

- Brazilian coffee: Brazil Santos Bourbon is a light bodied coffee, with low acidity, a pleasing aroma and a mild, smooth flavor.

- Jamaican coffee: The most common variety is Jamaican Blue Mountain coffee. Due to its limited production quantity, it is very expensive but has a rich flavor, intense aroma, full body and a smooth vibrant acidity.

THE PACIFIC: Includes coffees from Sumatra, Java, New Guinea and Sulawesi.

- Indonesian coffee: Java is the most famous Indonesian coffee and comes from the island of Java. This is a clean, thick, full body coffee with less of the earthy characteristics that other Indonesian coffees feature, such as Sumatra or Sulawesi. The Java coffees provide a smooth complement to the Yemen Mocha which is very intense. The traditional Mocha Java blend is the combination of Java and Yemen Mocha.

- Sumatran coffee: This coffee is a medium bodied coffee, low acid, sweet with a complex and earthy aroma.

brioche french toast stuffed with strawberries & cream

IF YOU WANT TO MAKE a breakfast that she (or he) will absolutely love, this is the one! The strawberry and cream cheese filling is a surprise that adds flavor and richness to what is already a decadent breakfast.

Makes 2 servings

Preheat oven to 350° F.

Let the cream cheese come to room temperature so it softens and will be easier to work with. Mince the strawberries and zest half the lemon. Mix with the cream cheese and honey until well incorporated.

Slice two very thick slices of bread from the loaf, at least 1 ½ to 2 inches thick. Using small sharp knife, cut a 2-inch-long slit in one side of each bread slice, cutting ¾ of way through bread and creating pocket that leaves three sides of bread intact. Gently stuff the cream cheese mixture into the pocket in the bread. You do not want to over stuff!

Whisk together eggs, milk, sugar, vanilla extract and a pinch of salt until blended. Pour into a deep baking pan and soak bread slices in 1 layer, turning once, 8 minutes. You want to give time for the egg mixture to soak into the thick slices.

Heat the butter in a skillet pan over moderately high heat until foam subsides. Transfer the soaked bread slices to the skillet with and cook until golden brown, about 1-2 minutes on each side. Transfer the skillet to the oven and cook for about 5-7 minutes. The French toast pieces will become slightly puffy (which is a good thing) and the center will be warmed through. Because the slices are thick and so rich, you will likely only need one slice each for you and your guest. Serve with maple syrup.

SHOPPING LIST

Unsliced brioche or challah bread, ½ loaf

Eggs, 2 large

Heavy cream, 2 tablespoons

Sugar, 1 teaspoon

Vanilla extract, ½ teaspoon

Butter, 3 tablespoons

Cream cheese, 4 ounces

Strawberries, ½ cup (if not in season, use frozen)

Lemon, 1 for zest

Honey, ½ teaspoon

Maple syrup

EQUIPMENT

Serrated knife

Large skillet pan

Deep baking dish

ginger scones with peach bellini jam

IF YOU WANT TO IMPRESS someone, this is the recipe to do that! This recipe lets you make a dozen scones. They freeze well and it helps to always keep a few in your freezer, you know, just in case …

the scones

Preheat oven to 400° F

Stir egg and cream together and set aside. In a separate large bowl, whisk flour, 2 tablespoons of sugar, baking powder and ¼ teaspoon of salt together in large bowl. Drop in butter in small pieces and using fingers (or a fork) work the butter into the flour until mixture resembles coarse meal. The pieces will range in size from pea size to oatmeal flakes and everything in between.

Make a well in the center and add egg and cream mixture. Using a fork, stir until just moist. Don't overdo it or your scones will be heavy like a bowling ball.

Cut the ginger into small pieces, no bigger than the size of an M&M candy. Transfer dough to floured work surface, sprinkle ginger pieces over top and gently knead until smooth, about 8 turns. Divide dough in half and shape each portion into ¾-inch-thick round. Cut each round into 6 wedges and transfer to baking sheet with silicone pad, spacing 1 inch apart. Brush tops with remaining 2 tablespoons cream and sprinkle with raw or baking sugar.

Bake scones until light brown, about 18-20 minutes. (These can be made one day ahead. Cool completely. Store in airtight container at room temperature. Re-warm in 350° F oven before serving.)

Makes 12 scones and enough jam for them

peach bellini jam

Defrost the peaches. In a pot, combine the peaches, 1 cup sugar, pinch of salt and juice from one lemon.

Bring to a boil then simmer for 25-30 minutes, stirring occasionally, until peaches fall apart. While they are cooking, break up the peaches with the back of a spoon or immersion blender. Meanwhile combine the cornstarch and 2 tablespoons of the sparkling wine in a small bowl. Using a wooden spoon stir the corn starch into the peach mixture and continue simmering for another 15 minutes, stir frequently. The peaches will have been almost completely broken down and the mixture will have a thick consistency. Remove from heat and add the remaining sparkling wine. Let the jam cool completely. Place in a covered container and refrigerate.

You can make the jam a day or a week in advance.

SHOPPING LIST

Frozen peaches, 2 pounds

Sugar, 1 cup plus 2 tablespoons

Lemon, 1 for juice

Cornstarch, 2 tablespoons

Sparkling wine, 4 tablespoons

Egg, 1 large

Heavy cream, ⅔ cup cold plus 2 tablespoons

Flour, 2 cups

Baking powder, 1 tablespoon

Butter, 5 tablespoons

Crystallized ginger, ¾ cup diced

Raw sugar, 2 tablespoons (or sugar with large crystals)

EQUIPMENT

Large pot (3 quart)

Wooden spoon

Baking sheet

Silicone non-stick pad

Immersion blender (optional)

low fat granola parfait

"It is worth spending the night just to be served this granola in the morning"
—A stunning PhD student

NOT ONLY IS THIS A healthy way to start the day, but the granola is addictive. Making your own granola may seem like a lot of work, but the flavor and texture is so much better than anything you will find in a store it is worth it! Baking the grain flakes/oats twice is what gives this granola the extra crunch and flavor. I included some of my favorite fruits, but you can easily substitute what is accessible or what looks best in the market.

Preheat the oven to 350° F. Combine the whole grain flakes with the almonds on a large rimmed baking sheet. Spread in an even layer and toast for about 10 minutes, stirring once, until light golden. Transfer the grain mixture to a large bowl. Leave the oven on.

In a bowl, combine the butter with the flour, sugar, cinnamon and salt and a pinch of salt and blend the ingredients together with your fingers until the mixture resembles coarse crumbs. Add the crumb mixture to the grain mixture and toss. In a small glass, combine the maple syrup, honey and vanilla. Pour over the grain mixture and stir until the grains are evenly moistened.

Spread the granola on the lined baking sheet in an even layer and toast for 14 to 16 minutes, stirring once, until very golden and dry. While you want to be careful it does not burn, you do want your granola to get dark, giving it tons of flavor and crunch. Let cool completely then stir in the dried blueberries and cranberries.

Makes two parfaits
and extra granola for a week

TO SERVE

Make the parfaits in the biggest wine glasses you have. Spoon 2 tablespoons of yogurt into the bottom of each glass and even out the surface. Spoon 2 tablespoons of granola over the top and smooth the surface. Spoon 2 tablespoons of fruit on top of the granola and smooth the surface. Repeat the process. Serve in bed with a smile.

Store the rest of the granola in an air-tight container and it keeps for a week.

SHOPPING LIST

Mixed organic whole grain flakes, 2 cups (look for a mix of oat, kamut, barley and wheat)

Sliced almonds, ½ cup

Butter, 2 tablespoons cold unsalted butter, cut into 6 pieces

Whole wheat flour, 3 tablespoons

Sugar, 1 tablespoon

Cinnamon, ½ teaspoon

Pure maple syrup, ¼ cup

Honey, ¼ cup

Vanilla extract, ½ teaspoon

Dried blueberries, ¼ cup

Dried cranberries, ¼ cup

Plain yogurt, 1 cup

Fresh seasonal berries, 1 cup (raspberries, blueberries, strawberries (hulled and sliced), and/or other fruit such as bananas or peaches sliced)

EQUIPMENT

Baking sheet

Non-stick silicone pad

Baking sheet

2 wine glasses or other tall glasses

Large mixing bowl

culinary notes

culinary notes

14 BRUNCH WITH THE IN-LAWS

... Pumpkin muffins with brown sugar creme filling

... Baked Eggs with Gruyere in prosciutto Cups

... Peaches in vanilla syrup over cinnamon yogurt

FEW THINGS ARE MORE STRESSFUL than entertaining for in-laws or potential in-laws. Starting with a champagne cocktail is a fun way to start any brunch and take the edge off.

Bellinis and Kir Royales are great alternatives to mimosas.

bellini

If peaches are in season, then puree fresh peaches, otherwise puree frozen peaches. You will need about 4 medium size peaches for every bottle of champagne.

Fill a champagne flute one third of the way with the peach puree and then fill the rest of the way with champagne.

SHOPPING LIST

Peaches

Champagne or prosecco

kir royale

Add a small amount of Chambord, about 1 ounce to a champagne flute and fill with champagne

SHOPPING LIST

Chambord (can substitute any raspberry or black currant liqueur)

Champagne

pumpkin muffins with brown sugar creme filling

THESE MUFFINS MAKE YOUR KITCHEN smell so amazing while baking that it will take a lot of self discipline not to eat all of them before your guests arrive. Their beautiful color, subtle spiciness and richness of the brown sugar cream cheese filling make these muffins addictive.

Heat oven to 400° F. Let the cream cheese come to room temperature.

In a mixing bowl combine one egg, vanilla extract, cream cheese, ½ cup of brown sugar and a pinch of salt. Blend until thoroughly combined and set aside in the refrigerator.

In a large mixing bowl combine the pumpkin puree, 1 egg, cream and ¼ cup brown sugar. Add flour, baking powder, baking soda, salt, cinnamon and nutmeg. When mixing in the dry ingredients, be gentle otherwise the muffins will become tough. Mix all ingredients just until flour is moistened, batter should be lumpy.

Makes 4 jumbo muffins

Fill the muffin cups ⅓ full with the batter. Place 1 teaspoon of the cream cheese mixture on top of the batter in each muffin cup and then add enough batter so the muffin cups are ⅔ full. Leave room for the muffins to rise during cooking. If you fill the muffin cup with batter to the top, it will overflow while cooking and make a brutal mess to clean up. Sprinkle a few walnut pieces over the top of each muffin.

Bake 18 to 20 minutes. To check if the muffins are done, stick a knife or toothpick in the muffin. It should have no orange batter sticking to it when you pull out the toothpick.

SHOPPING LIST

All purpose flour, 1 cup

Baking powder, 1 teaspoon

Baking soda, ¼ teaspoon

Salt, ¼ teaspoon

Ground cinnamon, ½ teaspoon

Ground nutmeg, ¼ teaspoon

Brown sugar, ¾ cup

Canned pumpkin puree, ¾ cup

Egg, 2 large

Cream, ¼ cup

Cream cheese, 4 ounces

Vanilla extract, 1 teaspoon

Chopped walnuts, ¼ cup

EQUIPMENT

Jumbo muffin pan (disposable with paper liners work great)

2 mixing bowls

baked eggs with gruyere in prosciutto cups

IT IS NICE TO BE able to serve your guests eggs without having to slave over the stove while they watch over your shoulder. This dish is simple to make, looks gorgeous on a plate and easy to scale up for any size crowd you have. Serve with some nice toast or biscuits to sop up the luscious yolks!

Preheat oven to 350° F.

Finely mince the garlic. Cut the tomato in half and use a finger to push out the seeds. When you are left with just the "meat" of the tomato, chop the tomato into small pieces. Finely chop chives, about 1 tablespoon or 8-10 chive stalks.

Heat the olive oil in the sauté pan over medium heat. Add minced garlic and spinach. Sauté until the spinach is cooked and the tomatoes are tender. Season with salt and pepper and set aside.

Spray the muffin pan with a vegetable spray to ensure the eggs will come out easily. Line each muffin cup with two pieces of prosciutto, ensuring the bottom is completely covered and it extends up to the top and slightly above the muffin cup. It should look the same as if a paper liner is in the muffin cup.

Makes 4 servings

SHOPPING LIST

Prosciutto, 8 slices

Egg, 4 large

Gruyere, 2 ounces

Fresh Spinach, 2 ounces

Tomato, 1 large

Garlic, 1 small clove

Olive oil, 1 tablespoon

Basil, 1 small bunch

Chives, 1 small bunch

EQUIPMENT

Muffin pan with large muffin cups (the disposable muffin pans works fine)

Small sauté pan

Spoon a heaping teaspoon of the spinach mixture into the bottom of each prosciutto lined muffin cup. Level off the mixture so that it is flat and not a round mound at the bottom of the cup. You want a level landing pad for the egg. Put two basil leaves on top of the spinach mixture. Crack the egg and gently drop the egg into the muffin cup. Top each egg with the gruyere cheese and chives evenly divided among the 4 muffin cups.

Bake in the preheated oven for 15-20 minutes until the egg whites are set. They are perfectly cooked when the egg whites are firm, but the yolk is still slightly runny in the middle. The prosciutto that extends above the egg will become nice and crispy. The prosciutto and eggs will easily come out of the muffin pan and are rich enough that guests will only need one for a satisfying breakfast.

peaches in vanilla syrup over cinnamon yogurt

THIS DESSERT HAS IT ALL — easy to make, looks great, incredibly aromatic with the vanilla and cinnamon and it tastes amazing! You will astonish your in-laws without breaking a sweat. If your in-laws are busy complimenting the food, they will have less time to ask about when will they start having grandchildren.

Stir yogurt and cinnamon together in a medium bowl. Cover and chill at least 1 hour or up to 1 day ahead.

Simmer wine, water and sugar over low heat. Using a sharp knife, cut the vanilla bean in half lengthwise, scrape the moist seeds in the middle and add them to the sugar, wine and water mixture.

While syrup is simmering, slice peaches into 6 slices per peach. It is easier if you purchase freestone peaches. As their name implies, the pit comes out easily. They are only available toward the end of peach season, mid to late summer. Otherwise, frozen peaches are a good substitute and will save you a step. Juice the lemon and toss the peaches with the lemon juice. This will stop the peaches from turning brown.

After 20 minutes, the sugar will be completely dissolved in the water/wine. The mixture should be reduced by half and it will begin to thicken. Remove from heat and pour hot syrup over the peaches. Make sure all of the peaches are thoroughly coated and let stand for 30 minutes.

Makes 4 servings

ASSEMBLY

Spoon chilled cinnamon yogurt into 4 dessert dishes. Spoon peaches and a small amount of syrup over the peaches. Sprinkle with pistachios.

SHOPPING LIST

Unflavored Greek yogurt, 1 ½ cups

Cinnamon, ¼ teaspoon ground

Dry white wine, ½ cup

Water, ½ cup

Sugar, ½ cup

Vanilla bean, 1 (or 2 teaspoons of vanilla extract)

Peaches, 4 medium size or ½ pound of frozen peaches

Lemon, 1 for juice

Pistachios, ½ cup

EQUIPMENT

2 medium size mixing bowls

4 small serving dishes

Small sauce pan

culinary notes

culinary notes

15
COCKTAIL PARTY FINGER FOOD

- Ginger scallops with candied jalapeños on wanton crisps
- Crispy olives stuffed with chicken and feta sausage
- Chipolte marshmallow crispy treats
- Miniature crab cakes with chive caper sauce
- Salmon in blankets with fried serrano cream
- Sweet potato, ham and leek frittata wedges with lemon aioli
- Tomato skewers with tequila vinaigrette
- Walnut, Arugula & Blue Cheese Crostini
- White chocolate spice cookies
- Rum balls

WHAT I LOVE ABOUT COCKTAIL parties is that you can experiment with a wide variety of eats and drinks. Guests will be grazing, mingling and drinking simultaneously.

Unless you have the time and money to stock a full bar, pick a few cocktails to serve and have plenty of wine and beer on hand. You do not need to buy a lot of equipment, a shaker with strainer and a blender will allow you to make most drinks.

By focusing on just a few cocktails to serve, you can buy higher quality alcohol and mixers. I like to change up the offerings between classics and funky new cocktails. Below are a few of my favorites:

classic martini

2 parts gin to ½ part dry vermouth. Mix well in a tall glass filled with ice, strain and pour into a glass with an olive. You can also make martinis by the pitcher.

SHOPPING LIST

- Gin (My personal favorites include Plymouth, Beefeater and Poodles)
- Dry Vermouth
- Stuffed olives (you can find olives stuffed with garlic, blue cheese, jalapeños besides the classic pimentos)

cosmopolitan

A gentleman does not make Cosmos. Ever.

Cocktail Party Finger Food

mojito

SHOPPING LIST

Light rum

fresh mint

sugar

sparkling water/ soda water

fresh lime juice

Take 3 sprigs of mint and vigorously mix with 2 teaspoons of sugar and a splash of soda water until the sugar has dissolved. Squeeze 1 ounce of lime juice in the mix and add 2 to 3 ounces of light rum. Shake this mixture up with ice and strain into a glass of ice. Top with another splash of soda water and a mint sprig.

death in the afternoon

ABSINTHE HAS ONLY BEEN LEGALLY sold in the US for a few years so there is still a fun novelty associated with this liquor.

SHOPPING LIST

Absinthe

Champagne

IN A CHAMPAGNE GLASS, FILL a quarter of the way with absinthe and the rest of the way with chilled champagne. The drink will turn a cool milky color.

ginger scallops on wonton crisps with candied jalapeño

THIS IS AN ELEGANT AND seductive hors d'oeurve. The subtle sweetness of the scallop is highlighted by the sweet heat of the candied jalapeño.

Makes 24 pieces, enough for 8-10 servings

Thinly slice the jalapeño peppers. Heat a sauté pan over medium-low heat and add ½ cup of water, sugar and pinch of salt. Stir until sugar is dissolved, add sliced peppers, and simmer 4 - 6 minutes. Take pan off heat and let the peppers cool in liquid. Set aside. The candied jalapeños can be made up to 2 days ahead.

Cut the wonton skins into rounds slightly larger than the diameter of the scallops. Use a glass or mug to outline the size you want to cut the wanton. Fry in hot vegetable oil until lightly brown and crisp. Let rest on a plate lined with paper towels to dry and sprinkle with salt.

Wipe the skillet clean and melt the butter. Dust one side of the scallops with a mixture of the flour and ginger powder. Place the scallops spiced-side down in the pan and sauté until brown and the center of the scallop is opaque. Do not crowd too many scallops in the skillet; cook them in smaller batches.

Arrange the scallops on the wonton skins and top with a candied jalapeño.

SHOPPING LIST

Vegetable oil, 2 cups

Large scallops, 12 halved horizontally

Wondra Flour, ½ cup (also known as instant flour)

Butter, ½ stick

Ground ginger, 2 teaspoons

Wonton skins, 25 (1 package)

Jalapeño peppers, 3

Sugar, ½ cup

EQUIPMENT

Large skillet or sauté pan

crispy olives stuffed with chicken & feta sausage

TALK ABOUT A FLAVOR PUNCH! They are crunchy, meaty, salty and cheesy all in one bite.

SHOPPING LIST

Ground chicken breast, 1 pound

Feta, 6 ounces

Dried sage, 1 tablespoon

Garlic chili sauce, ½ teaspoon

Spanish olives, 24 pitted large patted dry

vegetable oil, 2 cups (for frying)

All purpose flour, 1 cup

Egg, 1

Panko breadcrumbs, ½ cup

EQUIPMENT

mixing bowl

large skillet pan for frying

slotted spoon

Makes around 24 canapes

Mix the ground chicken breast, sage, pinch of salt and garlic chili sauce until evenly mixed. Cook mixture until cooked through and slightly browned. Let cool and mix in Feta cheese and blend until sausage is broken up into very fine pieces and the cheese is evenly incorporated. Remember that the sausage has to be small enough to fit into the olive.

Stuff olives with sausage and cheese mixture. Can be made 1 day ahead. Cover and chill.

Pour enough oil into heavy large skillet to measure depth of 1 inch and heat over medium high heat. Beat the egg and place in a small bowl. In two other bowls put the flour and panko bread crumbs. Roll stuffed olives in flour, then in egg, then in breadcrumbs to coat. Fry olives until golden brown on all sides, about 1 to 2 minutes. Using slotted spoon, transfer olives to paper towels to drain and sprinkle with salt. Serve warm.

chipotle marshmallow crispy treats

IT MIGHT SOUND LIKE CRAZY-TALK to make a savory version of this classic dessert, but try it once and you will be a convert. I came up with the idea for this recipe over pillow talk with another chef, it was a good night all around.

Makes 8-10 servings

In large saucepan, melt butter over low heat and blend in chipotle powder, paprika and salt. Add marshmallows, cranberries and stir until completely melted. Remove from heat.

Add cereal and stir until coated.

Spray the 13 x 9 inch pan with the vegetable spray so the mixture will not stick. Pour in the marshmallow rice krispie mixture and press firmly into the pan. Allow to completely cool. Cut into squares and serve.

SHOPPING LIST

Rice Krispies cereal, 6 cups

Marshmallows, 10 ounce package

Butter, 3 tablespoons

Chipotle chili powder, 2 tablespoons

Smoked paprika, 2 teaspoons

Dried cranberries, ⅔ cup

Salt, ½ teaspoon

EQUIPMENT

Large sauce pan

13 x 9 inch pan

Vegetable spray

miniature crab corn cakes with chive caper sauce

WHO DOESN'T LOVE CRAB CAKES? This elegant recipe will make anyone who eats them seem sophisticated.

dipping sauce

(Can be made 1 day ahead.)

To make the dipping sauce use a food processor to mix together 1 cup mayonnaise, leaves from ½ a bunch of parsley, ½ the shallot, juice from lemon, hot chili sauce and capers. Mix until the mixture becomes pale green and well blended. Transfer to small bowl. Drain the capers and stir in. Season to taste with salt and pepper. Cover and chill.

Makes 12-14 large servings

SHOPPING LIST

Mayonnaise, 1 ⅓ cups

Eggs, 2 yolks

Dijon mustard, 1 ½ tablespoons

Lemon, 1 for juice

Sriracha hot chili sauce, 1 teaspoon

Dried tarragon, ¾ teaspoon

Shallot, 1 large size

Canned corn, 4 ounces (pure corn, not one with any seasoning or sauce)

Blue crab finger crab meat, 1 pound (can substitute lump or jumbo lump crab)

Panko, 1 ½ cups

½ cup of vegetable oil

Fresh parsley, ¼ cup

Chives, about 12-15 leaves (that is the long slender hollow blade)

Lemon, 1 for juice

Hot pepper sauce, ½ teaspoon

Capers, 2 tablespoons

EQUIPMENT

Food processor

Mixing bowl

Skillet pan

baking sheet

crab cakes

To make the crab cakes, finely mince the other ½ of the shallot and chives. In a bowl whisk together ⅓ cup mayonnaise, egg yolks, mustard, lemon juice, tarragon and chile sauce. Gently stir in crab, corn and salt and pepper to taste. You do not want to break up the big beautiful pieces of crab. Chill the crab mixture, covered, at least 1 hour or up to 1 day.

In a large shallow plate spread out panko bread crumbs. Form rounded teaspoons of crab mixture into slightly flattened 1-inch rounds and gently coat with panko, transferring to a baking sheet. Chill crab cakes, loosely covered with wax paper, at least 2 hours or up to 4.

Heat ¼ cup of oil in heavy large skillet over medium heat. Working in batches, add crab cakes to skillet and cook until golden brown on both sides and heated through, about 2 minutes per side. Add more oil as necessary. Transfer the crab cakes to paper towel-lined plate to drain off any oil.

Serve on a large platter with the bowl of dipping sauce.

Cocktail Party Finger Food

salmon in blankets with fried serrano cream

THIS RECIPE IS GUARANTEED TO astonish guests, just do not tell them how simple it is! No matter how many pieces are made, I am quickly staring at an empty platter. The final product will resemble the classic kids dish "pigs in a blanket", miniature hot dogs wrapped in dough. By the time the puff pastry is baked, the salmon will be cooked to a perfect medium, leaving it velvety moist. Let your fish monger do all the hard work by removing the skin and bones from the salmon.

fried serrano cream

SHOPPING LIST

Canola oil, 6 ounces

Serrano chilies, 6 chilies

White onion, one medium size

A garlic clove

Heavy cream, ½ cup

EQUIPMENT

Blender or immersion blender

Frying pan

Heat oil in medium saucepan over medium-high heat. When the oil is hot enough, you will see the surface shimmer and the chile should sizzle as soon as they are dropped in the oil. Fry chilies until blistered, about 3 minutes. Remove chilies from oil. Cool chilies completely.

Cut the onion in half and peel and roughly chop one half. Add onion and garlic clove to the pan and cook until softened and well browned, about 7-10 minutes. Set aside onion and garlic to cool and RESERVE the oil.

Cut stems off chilies. If you want to reduce the heat level of the sauce, remove the seeds. Combine chilies, onions, garlic, pinch of salt, and oil used in frying the chilies and onions in blender and blend until the mixture has a smooth consistency. This can be made up to two days in advance and stored in the refrigerator.

Makes 12-14 servings

salmon in blankets

THIS DISH CAN BE PREPPED a few hours in advance and covered in the refrigerator, then put in the oven when your guest arrive.

Take the butter and the frozen puff pastry out of the refrigerator and let them come to room temperature.

Mince the two shallots into very fine pieces. You should have around four tablespoons. Remove the tarragon leaves from the stems and chop the leaves into small pieces. Thoroughly mix together the room temperature butter with the minced shallots and chopped tarragon. Season with salt and pepper to taste.

Pat the salmon dry and cut into rectangles about 1 inch by 2 inches. Because fish are not shaped like perfect rectangles, there will be some irregular shaped pieces. Try to have the pieces as uniform as possible so that they all cook evenly.

Preheat oven to 425° F.

Cut the sheet of puff pastry into long strips about 1 ½ wide. The strips should be slightly narrower than the salmon pieces. Cut each strip into about 5 pieces. Each strip should be just long enough to wrap around a piece of salmon. Since the salmon pieces should be slightly longer than the pastry, the ends will just barely stick out. To assemble, place about ½ teaspoon of the shallot butter mixture on a piece of salmon and wrap with a piece of pastry. Firmly pinch the ends of the pastry together to seal.

SHOPPING LIST

Frozen puff pastry, 1 package with 2 sheets 17.3-ounce

Salmon filets, 1 ½ pounds with the skin and pin bones removed.

Shallots, 2

Fresh tarragon, 4 stems (if you must, substitute 2 teaspoons of dried tarragon)

Butter, 8 ounces

EQUIPMENT

Sheet pan

Silicone non-stick pad

Sharp knife or pizza cutter

Place the wrapped salmon pieces, edge side down, on a cooking sheet lined with a silicone pad or parchment paper to prevent the pieces from sticking.

Bake pastries until pastry is golden brown, about 15-20 minutes. Remove from oven and let stand 10 minutes and serve while still warm.

Cocktail Party Finger Food

sweet potato, ham and leek frittata wedges with lemon aioli

THIS COLORFUL AND TASTY FRITTATA is one of my favorite finger foods to make for guests. Since it can be made in advance and served at room temperature this dish is very host friendly. You can make the frittata hours before the guests arrive.

aioli

Make the aioli up to 3 days in advance.

Finely mince the garlic and finely chop six chive pieces. Mix together the garlic, chives mayonnaise and olive oil. Season with salt and pepper and refrigerate until ready to use.

frittata

Make the frittata the day of the party.

Preheat oven to 325° F.

Peel the sweet potatoes and cut into small half-inch cubes. Place the cubes in a microwave friendly bowl and microwave for 4-6 minutes, until they are soft but not falling apart.

Cut the leek in half, the long way, using the root end to keep each half from falling apart. Carefully rinse under running water, making sure to rinse between layers where dirt sometimes accumulates. Thinly slice the white and pale green part of the leek and discard the dark green part.

Makes 16 hors d'oeuvres size servings

Heat a 10-inch, non-stick skillet over medium heat. Melt the butter and add the leeks. Cook until the leeks are tender, 6-7 minutes. Dice the ham into small pieces. Add the ham, sweet potato cubes and season with salt and pepper.

In a mixing bowl, beat eggs together so they are thoroughly mixed and add a splash of hot sauce along with some salt and pepper. Pour the egg mixture into the pan. Stir everything around so the eggs are evenly mixed with the ham, potatoes and leeks. Place the skillet into the pre-heated oven for 20-25 minutes. You will know it is done when the center is firm and the frittata is puffed and golden.

It can be served warm or at room temperature. Using a plate that is at least as large as the skillet, flip the frittata onto the plate and slice into 16 thin slices. Place a small dollop of aioli on top of each slice.

SHOPPING LIST

Butter, 4 tablespoons

Sweet potatoes or yams, two medium size. about 1 ½ pounds

Eggs, 8

Hot sauce, a splash (use your favorite brand)

Ham, 4 ounces (use any ham you like, just have the deli counter cut thick slices)

Leek, 1

Garlic, 3 cloves

Chives, 1 small bunch

Mayonnaise, ½ cup

Olive oil, 1 tablespoon

EQUIPMENT

10-inch non-stick skillet

Mixing bowl

Microwave oven

Spatula

tomato skewers with tequila vinaigrette

THIS VEGETARIAN HORS D'OEURVE PACKS a punch with its tequila vinaigrette. It is important to have healthier snack options available for your guests and this is both healthy and delicious. Since the alcohol does not cook out of the vinaigrette, guests that eat more than three might need a designated driver.

tequila vinaigrette

Juice the grapefruit into a small mixing bowl, watch out for seeds. Add the tequila and mustard to the grapefruit juice and whisk together. After the mustard, grapefruit and tequila are thoroughly mixed together, slowly add the olive oil while continuing to whisk the mixture. Season with salt and pepper to taste. The vinaigrette can be made a few days in advance, just keep refrigerated.

Makes 8-10 servings

Wash and dry the tomatoes. Pick off the leaves from the mint stems and throw out the stems.

When ready to serve, dice the avocados. Cut the avocados on half and discard the pit. Use a spoon to scoop out the flesh in one large piece. Dice the avocados into pieces approximately the same size as the cherry tomatoes.

In a large mixing bowl combine the tomatoes, avocado cubes and mint leaves. Pour in the dressing and gently mix to coat everything. Place one tomato, mint leaf and an avocado cube on a single toothpick and repeat until all the tomatoes and avocados are skewered. Assembling this dish will be a little messy because the vegetables have dressing on them, so have paper towels handy. Place the skewers on a large platter and use any extra mint leaves to garnish.

SHOPPING LIST

Cherry tomatoes, 1 pint

Avocados, 3 (they should be ripe but not mushy)

Tequila, blanco, 1 ounce

Grapefruit, 1 large

Olive oil, 5 ounces

Mint, 1 bunch

Dijon mustard, 1 teaspoon

EQUIPMENT

Tooth picks

Mixing bowl

walnut, arugula and blue cheese crostini

THIS IS A WINE FRIENDLY treat that everyone will love. It is perfect for cocktail party grazing.

Preheat oven to 400° F. and let the butter come to room temperature. Cut the baguette into thin slices about ¼ inch thick.

Spread butter over 1 side of each baguette slice. Arrange baguette slices on baking sheet, butter side up. Bake baguette slices until golden, about 12 minutes. Cool.

Reduce oven temperature to 350° F.

Finely chop the arugula. Mix walnuts, gorgonzola, honey, olive oil and arugula in medium bowl. Season with salt and pepper. Spoon nut-cheese mixture evenly atop baguette toasts, pressing to adhere. Bake toasts just until cheese melts, about 6 minutes. Let the crostini cool so they do not burn the mouths of your guests.

Makes around 18 canapés

SHOPPING LIST

Butter, 8 ounces

Baguette, 1

Walnuts, 6 tablespoons

Gorgonzola cheese, 3 ounces (you can substitute other blue cheeses)

Olive oil, 1 tablespoon

Honey, 1 teaspoon

Arugula, 3 tablespoons

Cherry tomatoes

EQUIPMENT

Baking sheet

Non-stick silicone pad

Cocktail Party Finger Food

white chocolate spice cookies

NOT ONLY DO THESE COOKIES look cool, but they have great flavor and texture. The subtle spiciness in the cookies along with the white chocolate makes these a sinfully grown up cookie.

Preheat oven to 325° F.

You can mix everything by hand but it is so much easier to make the recipe using a food processor. Cut the butter into ½ inch pieces. In a food processor mix together at a slow speed the flour, sugar, ginger, pepper, baking soda, cocoa powder, cinnamon, allspice, and salt. Slowly add the butter one or two pieces at a time until mixture resembles coarse meal.

Zest the lemon; you should have about 2 teaspoons worth of zest. In a small bowl, mix together vanilla, lemon peel and 1 tablespoon water. Add to food processor or bowl; whirl or stir until dough forms a ball.

Place the dough in the middle of a large sheet of wax paper. Fold the wax paper over the dough and start to form dough into a log. Work the dough so it becomes an even and smooth cylinder. Place the dough into the refrigerator and chill rolled dough until firm, about 45 minutes (or freeze about 25 minutes).

Slice the log into ½ inch slices and place on a baking sheet lined with a non-stick pad or parchment paper. Place ½ inch apart; they will spread out slightly while cooking.

Makes 12-14 servings

Bake cookies in a 325° oven until pale brown, about 15 minutes. Transfer to racks to cool completely.

To melt the white chocolate, place white chocolate and vegetable oil in a heatproof bowl set over a pan of barely simmering water (bottom of bowl should not touch water). Stir until chocolate is melted and mixture is smooth. Take off heat.

Dip each cookie about two-thirds of the way into white chocolate mixture, then place on a baking sheet lined with waxed paper. Set aside and let the chocolate glaze harden.

While the white chocolate glaze is hardening, melt the semisweet chocolate using the same method.

When the semisweet chocolate is melted and smooth, use a fork to drizzle the chocolate over the cookies in a random pattern....imagine what the artist Jackson Pollock would do. Let the chocolate harden.

The cookies can be stored in an airtight container for a few days. Place wax paper between the layers of cookies so they do not stick together.

SHOPPING LIST

All-purpose flour, 2 cups

Light brown sugar, ⅔ cup firmly packed

Ground ginger, 1 teaspoon

Fresh-ground pepper, ¾ teaspoon

Baking soda, ½ teaspoon

Unsweetened cocoa powder, ½ teaspoon

Ground cinnamon, ¼ teaspoon

Ground allspice, ½ teaspoon

Salt, healthy pinch

Butter, 1 cup (½ lb.) unsalted butter

Vanilla extract, 1 teaspoon

Lemon, 1 for zest

White chocolate chips or pieces, 6 ounces

Vegetable oil, 1 teaspoon

Semi-sweet chocolate chips or pieces, 2 ounces

EQUIPMENT

Food processor

Lemon zester

Wax paper

Baking sheet

Non-stick silicone pad or parchment paper

Metal mixing bowl to use as a double boiler

rum balls

SOMETIMES THE MOST POPULAR DESSERTS are ones that you can just pop in your mouth, no utensils needed. This dessert combines rum and chocolate into moist nuggets for a luxurious treat that can be made a few days in advance.

Preheat oven to 350° F.

Place the pecans on a baking sheet and toast until lightly browned and fragrant, 8-12 minutes. Let cool completely and then place in your food processor and pulse until finely chopped. Transfer to a large bowl.

Mix together half-cup of the confectioners' sugar and cocoa powder.

Process the vanilla wafer cookies in the food processor until finely ground. Add the crumbs to the finely chopped pecans. To this mixture add the sugar and cocoa powder and stir until combined. Add the corn syrup and rum and mix well. Refrigerate for 30 minutes so the mixture will firm up and be easier to work with. Use a tablespoon to scoop out a small amount of the mixture and shape into one inch balls using your hands.

Place the remaining half-cup of confectioners' sugar into a small bowl and roll the rum balls in the sugar to evenly coat.

Store in an airtight container in the refrigerator. These are best if made several days in advance of serving to allow the flavors to mingle.

Serve at room temperature.

Makes around 24 balls, enough for about 8 guests

SHOPPING LIST

Pecans, 1 ½ cups (can substitute hazelnuts, walnuts, or almonds)

Vanilla wafer cookies, 1 ¼ cups (can substitute meringues, ginger cookies or chocolate wafers)

Confectioners' sugar, 1 cup

Unsweetened cocoa powder, 2 tablespoons

Light corn syrup, 2 tablespoons

Dark rum, ¼ cup (can substitute bourbon)

EQUIPMENT

Food processor

Baking sheet

Cocktail Party Finger Food

culinary notes

culinary notes

16 POKER NIGHT WITH THE BOYS

... Duck confit jalapeño poppers

... Pumpkin seed crusted chicken bites with chipotle yogurt dipping sauce

... Texas chili

... Winners buttermilk pie

IF YOU ARE HAVING THE guys over for poker or couples over for game night, you will need to feed them and these recipes will let you amaze them.

TOP FIVE WAYS TO GET SHOT WHILE PLAYING POKER:

- Do not reveal your cards while a hand is going on. Even if it is an accident, you should be apologizing your ass off.

- If you folded and your cards would have made a great hand on the flop, don't reel back in your chair or bang your hand off of the table or let your stupid jaw hang open, letting everyone know that you would have hit that flop. In fact, don't react to the cards on the board at all.

- Don't be mean by criticizing an opponent's play, being verbally abusive to another player, or by being cocky about how good you think you are.

- Don't blame the dealer. Also, don't wing your cards at the dealer or not tip him as a result of a previous bad beat.

- Do not talk about a hand when you aren't in it. The players who are still in the hand don't want to have to listen to your noise pollution when they're trying to focus on the other live opponents. So shut yer mouth.

duck confit jalapeño poppers

THE RICH SUCCULENCE OF THE duck confit and the bite of the jalapeño pepper is a perfect marriage. Duck confit sounds exotic, but it is very easy to make. Similar to barbeque, it is cooked slowly at a low temperature. The bonus with this dish is the leftover duck fat. Use the fat to fry any kind of potatoes, a classic treat often found in Parisian bistros.

In a small bowl, combine salt, pepper, thyme and bay leaf. Place duck legs, fat side down, in a pan in one layer and sprinkle duck generously with mixture. The duck legs should fit snugly in the pan; if necessary use 2 smaller pans. Cover tightly with plastic wrap and refrigerate for 24 hours.

The next day, pre-heat oven to 325º F. and remove the duck from the refrigerator and let come to room temperature, about 20 minutes. Flip the duck legs so the fat is on top. Add the olive oil and over medium high heat on the cook top, cook the duck legs until the fat on the duck starts to render. You will know the duck fat is beginning to render when you hear it sizzle. After about 15 minutes, cover pan with lid (or foil), and place it in oven.

Roast legs for 3 hours. The meat should easily fall off the bone. Remove duck from fat and reserve fat for other uses.* The fat will keep in the refrigerator for a few days or the freezer for a few months.

*Do not throw out the duck fat! You can use the reserved duck fat to roast potatoes or cook hash browns for an incredible treat.

Makes 6 servings

SHOPPING LIST

Freshly ground black pepper, ½ teaspoon

Dried thyme, ½ teaspoon

Bay leaf, 1

Moulard duck legs, 4 (about 2 pounds total)

Olive oil, 1 cup

Salt, 1 teaspoon

Grated parmesan cheese, 4 ounces

Jalapeño peppers, 12

EQUIPMENT

Medium size skillet with a lid

Baking sheet

Set aside the meat and dispose of the bones and skin. When the meat cools, the meat should pull apart into large chunks. It will have the same texture as pulled pork. Roughly chop the duck meat into pieces about the size of your thumb, the meat should be able to fit in the jalapeño halves. Mix the meat with the parmesan cheese and add ground pepper to taste. The cheese should add enough saltiness that extra salt will not be needed.

Cut the jalapeño in half lengthwise. Scrape out the seeds so you are left with a hollow jalapeño half. Arrange the peppers on cookie sheet, transfer to the oven and roast for 20 minutes. The peppers will soften and the duck/cheese mixture will begin to brown. Serve immediately.

pumpkin seed crusted chicken bites with chipotle yogurt dipping sauce

THE PUMPKIN SEED CRUST GIVES this dish a wonderfully distinctive look and taste. It is equally delicious served warm or at room temperature.

SHOPPING LIST

Greek style yogurt, 14 ounces

Chipotle peppers in adobo sauce

Lime, 1

Honey, ½ teaspoon

chipotle yogurt dipping sauce

Finely chop 2 chipotle peppers and reserve 1 teaspoon of the adobo sauce that they come in. Zest the lime.

Mix together all of the ingredients and season with salt and pepper to taste. The sauce can be made up to two days in advance.

Makes 6-8 servings

Preheat oven to 425º F.

Place the seeds on the baking sheet and toast them in the oven for 10 minutes. They will gain a little color and become fragrant. You do not want the seeds to darken. Set aside to cool.

Place the pumpkin seeds in a plastic bag and then using a heavy bottom pan crush the seeds into to smaller pieces. The seeds should be broken up, but still in big pieces. You do not want to smash them so hard that they resemble breadcrumbs or that the bag breaks and you are sweeping them off the floor.

Cut each tender into 3 pieces. Remove the leaves from the thyme and finely chop.

In a mixing bowl combine the toasted pumpkin seeds, ancho powder, thyme and salt. In a separate bowl whisk the 2 eggs with ½ cup of water. Put the flour in a shallow bowl and season with salt and pepper. Dredge the chicken tender pieces in flour and then dip in the egg and then into the mixing bowl with the pumpkin seeds. Press firmly to ensure pumpkin seeds firmly adhere to the chicken.

Place the coated chicken pieces on a baking sheet lined with the silicone pad or parchment paper. Bake for 15-20 minutes or until the chicken is cooked though. Place on a platter with toothpicks in each piece so guests can easily pick them up. Serve with chipotle yogurt dipping sauce.

SHOPPING LIST

Raw unsalted pumpkin seeds, 2 cups (shelled)

Ancho powder, 1 teaspoon

Eggs, 2 large

Fresh thyme, 1 teaspoon

Salt, 1 teaspoon

Chicken tenders, 2 pounds

Extra-virgin olive oil, 2 tablespoons

All Purpose flour, 2 cups

EQUIPMENT

Baking sheet

Silicone non-stick pad or parchment paper

Mixing bowl

2 shallow bowls

Toothpicks for serving

texas chili

CHILI FIRST BECAME POPULAR IN Texas in the 1880's with the San Antonio "Chili Queens". Original versions of Chili contained only meat and chili peppers. Over the years, tomatoes, onions, garlic and beans joined the party along with chopped onions and grated cheese as garnishes. Cooking the beans separately helps ensure both the chili and the beans are both cooked to perfect doneness.

EQUIPMENT

Large skillet

Large pot, at least 8 quart in size

Kitchen scissors (optional)

Cook the bacon in a large skillet until crisp.

While the bacon is cooking, roughly chop one onion and cut the beef into ½ inch cubes. While cubing the beef, trim away excess fat. Mince 4 garlic cloves and the jalapeño pepper. Cut up the dried chipotle chilies into small pieces (using kitchen scissors makes fast work of this).

Remove the bacon and reserve the fat in the pan. Over high heat, brown the beef in the bacon drippings left in the skillet. When cooked removed the meat and set aside. Over medium heat, sauté the onions in the remaining drippings for 8-10 minutes, until lightly browned.

To the sautéing onions, add the cumin, ancho chili, smoked paprika, minced jalapeño, oregano, black pepper, thyme, salt, and minced garlic and sauté for 3 more minutes. The spices will become very fragrant. Crumble in the bacon; add the beer, broth, tomatoes, chipotle chilies, corn starch and the beef (including any juices that were released while the beef was resting). Bring to a boil then reduce the heat, cover partially, and simmer for 2 ½ to 3 hours or until the meat is very tender.

Makes 6 servings (or 2 for Texans)

SHOPPING LIST

Bacon, ¼ pound about 6 slices)

Chuck steak or Brisket, 3 pounds

Onions, 3 large ones

Ground cumin, 1 tablespoon

Ancho chili powder, 3 tablespoons

Smoked paprika, 2 teaspoons

Dried Mexican oregano, 1 teaspoon

Ground black pepper, 1 teaspoon

Dried thyme, ½ teaspoon

Salt, ½ teaspoon

Jalapeño pepper, 1

One bottle of beer, preferably Shiner Bock

Beef broth, 8 ounces

Chopped tomatoes, one 28-ounce can

Dried chipotle chilies, 2

Corn starch, 1 tablespoon

Carrots, 2

Celery, 2 stalks

Garlic, 6 cloves

Olive oil, 2 tablespoons

Bay leaf

Grated cheddar cheese, 8 ounces

Beans, one pound pinto or dried Yellow Indian Woman beans from www.ranchogordo.com

Cook the Beans

I think the creaminess of the Yellow Indian Woman beans is a great contrast to the rich spicy flavor of the Chili and the color contrasts look awesome. Pinto beans also work very well. You can purchase pinto beans already cooked and skip this step.

Roughly chop one onion, carrots 2 garlic cloves and celery and sauté in the olive oil. In a large pot, add the sautéed vegetables, a bay leaf, the beans and enough water to cover the beans by 2 inches.

Bring to a boil over medium high heat and let it boil for 5 minutes then reduce to a very low heat and let it simmer. Your nose will tell you when the beans are almost ready and the wonderful smell is the hint that this is the time to add a little salt.

Before serving, mince the remaining onion.

To serve add beans and chili to individual bowls and garnish with minced onions and cheese.

winners buttermilk pie

I HAD NEVER EVEN HEARD of buttermilk pie until I moved to Texas, and my life has not been the same since! One of the great things about this pie, besides the amazing flavor and texture, is that it can be served warm, room temperature or cold. The lushness of the custard is balanced by the fruit and bourbon in the pie.

Preheat the oven to 325° F. Melt the butter in the microwave and let cool. Separate the egg whites and yolks and set aside the yolks. Zest the lemon.

Defrost the pie crust according to package directions.

In a bowl whisk together the butter, sugar, buttermilk, egg yolks, flour, vanilla, bourbon, zest, salt, and nutmeg and pour the filling into the shell. Sprinkle the fruit evenly across the top of the filling. Place the filled pie shell on the baking sheet so it will be easier to handle and the sheet will capture any spillover.

Bake the pie for 40 to 50 minutes, or until the filling is set and golden. The center of the pie should just start to become firm. Let the pie cool on a rack and serve it at room temperature or chilled. You can bake the pie up to a day in advance and let it come to room temperature for ½ hour before serving.

Makes 6-8 servings

SHOPPING LIST

Butter, ½ stick (¼ cup)

Sugar, 1 cup

Buttermilk, 1 ½ cups

Eggs, 4

All-purpose flour, 4 tablespoons

Vanilla, 1 teaspoon

Lemon, 1

Salt, ¼ teaspoon

Freshly grated nutmeg to taste

Bourbon, ½ ounce

Fresh seasonal berries, like raspberries or blueberries, 3 ounces

Unbaked frozen 10-inch basic pie crust shell

EQUIPMENT

10 inch pie pan (not necessary if the pie crust comes in an aluminum pan)

Zester

Baking sheet

culinary notes

SHOPPING LIST INDEX

Tear out and take these cheat sheets with you to the store.

SCOTCH TASTING AFFAIR   14

walnut chutney   17

SHOPPING LIST

- ❏ Golden Delicious apple, 1 medium
- ❏ Shallot, 1 medium
- ❏ Jalapeño, 1
- ❏ Chopped walnuts, ⅔ cup
- ❏ Golden raisins, ⅔ cup
- ❏ Dark brown sugar, ¾ cup firmly packed
- ❏ Ground cinnamon, 1 teaspoon
- ❏ Ground ginger, ½ teaspoon
- ❏ Orange zest, ½ teaspoon
- ❏ Ground allspice, ¼ teaspoon
- ❏ Red-pepper flakes, ¼ teaspoon
- ❏ Hot sauce, 3-4 splashes
- ❏ Apple Juice, ½ cup
- ❏ Apple cider vinegar, ½ cup

duck prosciutto with walnut chutney   18

SHOPPING LIST

- ❏ Kosher salt, 4 cups
- ❏ Sugar, 2 cups
- ❏ Juniper berries, 10
- ❏ Bay leaf
- ❏ Fresh ground pepper, 2 teaspoons
- ❏ Magret boneless duck breast halves, 2 (a total of 8 ounces)

smoked trout rillettes   20

SHOPPING LIST

- ❏ Smoked trout, about 7 ounces which will produce 1 ½ cups when the skin and bones are removed. (Can substitute hot smoked salmon if you cannot find trout.)
- ❏ Mascarpone cheese, 4 ounces
- ❏ Butter, 3 tablespoons (room temperature)
- ❏ Green onion, about 2 stalks
- ❏ Shallot, 1 medium size
- ❏ Lemon, 1 large
- ❏ Splash of hot sauce
- ❏ Assorted crackers or a sliced baguette

prime rib bites with mustard cream sauce   22

SHOPPING LIST

- ❏ Rib-eye steaks, 2 thick steaks, about 1 inch thick
- ❏ Garlic, 2 cloves
- ❏ Rosemary, 3-4 branches
- ❏ Vegetable oil, 1 cup
- ❏ Sour cream, 1 cup
- ❏ Dijon mustard, 1 cup
- ❏ Honey, 1 teaspoon
- ❏ Lemon, 1 small for zest

risotto scotch eggs 24

SHOPPING LIST

- Eggs, 8
- Mild Italian sausage, 8 ounces
- Panko bread crumbs, 16 ounces
- Butter, 5 tablespoons
- Small onion, 1
- Garlic clove, 1
- Arborio rice, 1 pound
- Dry white wine, 1 cup
- Low-salt chicken broth, 6 cups
- Grated Parmesan cheese, 6 cups
- Vegetable oil spray

dark chocolate tart with pretzel crust 26

SHOPPING LIST

- Unsalted butter 4 ounces (one stick)
- Thin pretzels, 4 ounces or about 1 ¾ cups
- Confectioners' sugar ¾ cup
- All-purpose flour ½ cup
- Egg, 1
- Heavy cream 1 ½ cups
- Bittersweet chocolate, 12 ounces, morsel or chopped. If you have options, pick a dark chocolate in the 60-70% cocoa range.
- Any dried beans, 2 cups (they are not for eating and you will throw them out after using them)

SUPER BOWL/MARCH MADNESS 30

tomatillo guacamole salsa 32
SHOPPING LIST
- Tomatillos, 1 pound
- Cilantro, 1 bunch
- Garlic, 2 cloves
- Ripe avocados, 3
- Serrano peppers, 4
- Limes, 3 for juice
- Tortilla chips or corn tortillas

edamame dip 33
SHOPPING LIST
- Edamame, 12 ounces pre-cooked
- Onion, 1 small
- Cilantro, ½ bunch
- Garlic, 1 large clove
- Lemons, 2 for juice
- Brown miso, 1 tablespoon *(optional)
- Red chili paste, 1 tablespoon (or to taste)
- Olive oil, 5 tablespoons
- Honey ½ tablespoon
- Tortilla chips or pita bread

pork, pork, pork and sauerkraut stew 34
SHOPPING LIST
- Dried porcini mushrooms, ¼ ounce
- Thick cut bacon, 1/2 pound
- Smoked pork chops, 1 pound
- Smoked kielbasa, 1/2 pound
- Allspice, 2 teaspoons
- Dry mustard, 1 teaspoon
- Bay leaves, 2
- Yellow onions, 2 large
- Tomato paste, 4.5 ounces (one tube)
- Sauerkraut, 4 pounds
- White wine, 2 cups (use a fruity white wine with no oak)
- Low Sodium chicken stock, 1 cup

bison lollipops in dried cherry sauce 36

SHOPPING LIST

- Bison, 2 pounds ground
- Salt, 2 teaspoons
- Ground pepper, 2 teaspoons
- Shallot, 1
- Garlic, 2 cloves
- Garlic chili paste, 3 tablespoons
- Dried thyme, 1 teaspoon
- Egg, 1 large
- Vegetable oil, 3 tablespoons
- Onion, 1 small
- Tomato paste, 2 tablespoons
- Dried cherries, 9 ounces
- Bay leaf, 1
- Fresh thyme, 2 sprigs
- Red wine, 1 cup
  Merlot or Malbec work great
- Balsamic vinegar, 3 tablespoons
- Low sodium chicken broth, 22 ounces

turkey sliders with chipotle thousand island dressing 38

SHOPPING LIST

- Ground turkey, 1 ½ pounds (dark meat or a combination of white and dark meat)
- Shallot, 1 large
- Vegetable oil, 2 tablespoons
- Garlic chili paste, 2 tablespoons
- Parmesan cheese, 2 ounces
- Vegetable oil, 1 tablespoon
- Extra-sharp Cheddar, 8 slices, (5 ounces)
- Small rolls, 8
- Low-fat mayonnaise, 1 cup
- Ketchup, 2 tablespoons
- Lemon, 1 for juice
- Sweet pickle relish, 1 tablespoon
- Dijon mustard, 2 tablespoons
- Chipotle peppers in adobo sauce, small can

italian macaroni pie 40

SHOPPING LIST

- Vegetable oil, 2 tablespoons
- Butter, 1 tablespoon
- Porchetta*, 1 ¼ pound (can substitute ham)
- Carrot, 1 small
- Onion, 1
- Red wine, 1 ½ cups
- Dry basil, 1 tablespoon
- Jar of quality tomato sauce, 24 ounces
- Ziti, 1 ½ pounds
- Fresh ricotta, 1 pound
- Frozen chopped spinach, 1 pound
- Provolone cheese, 8 ounces
- Parmigiano-reggiano, ½ cup grated

"jambalaya" bread pudding 42

SHOPPING LIST

- High quality white bread or an "eggy" bread such as brioche or Challah, 2 unsliced loaves
- Andouille sausages or other fully cooked smoked spicy sausages (such as Louisiana hot links), 1 pound
- Medium size shrimp (31/40), ¾ of a pound. It is easier if they are purchased peeled and de-veined.
- Chicken meat, ½ pound. The dark meat from roasted chicken you find in supermarkets works well. If you can find Tasso, the spicy ham, that would be a great substitution for the chicken!
- Lemon, 1
- Eggs, 5
- White wine (anything but Chardonnay) or pilsner-style ale, 4 ounces
- Whole milk, 1 cup
- Heavy cream, 3 cups
- Butter, 5 tablespoons
- Yellow onion, 1 medium yellow chopped
- Red bell pepper, 1 chopped into small pieces
- Green onions, 5 stalks with just the green part thinly sliced
- Celery, 1 stalk sliced
- Garlic, 5 cloves finely chopped
- Dried cayenne pepper, 2 teaspoons
- Dried thyme, 1 teaspoon (or 2 teaspoons fresh thyme)
- Hot sauce (optional)
- Worcestershire sauce, 1 teaspoon
- Can of diced tomatoes (14 ½ ounce), drained of the juice
- Parmesan cheese, 4 ounces grated

sweet potato salad with mustard greens and bacon vinaigrette 44

SHOPPING LIST

- Red wine vinegar, 3 tablespoons
- Dijon mustard, 3 tablespoons
- Honey, 1 ½ tablespoons
- Hot sauce, 7-8 splashes (1 ½ teaspoons hot pepper sauce)
- Lemon, 1 for juice
- Olive oil, 7 tablespoons
- Sweet potatoes, 2 pounds
- Bacon, 6 slices
- Mustard greens, 10 large leaves (you can substitute kale, Swiss chard or turnip greens)

sinful vanilla bourbon rice pudding 46

SHOPPING LIST

- Whole milk, 1 ½ quarts
- Sugar, ⅔ cup
- Long grain rice, ½ cup
- Raisins, ½ cup
- Cinnamon, 1 stick
- Vanilla extract, 2 teaspoons
- Bourbon, ½ cup
- Heavy cream, ½ cup

CHEESE AND WINE PARTY 50

paprika candied pecans 53

SHOPPING LIST

- ❑ Maple syrup, 1 ½ tablespoons
- ❑ Honey, 1 ½ tablespoons
- ❑ Salt, ¾ teaspoon
- ❑ Freshly ground black pepper, ¼ teaspoon
- ❑ Cayenne pepper, 1 teaspoon
- ❑ Cinnamon, ½ teaspoon
- ❑ Smoked paprika, 1 teaspoon
- ❑ Raw pecan pieces, 2 cups

garlic and thyme marinated warmed olives 54

SHOPPING LISTS

- ❑ Olives, 1 pound of a variety such as Kalamata or Picholine (about 3 cups)
- ❑ Garlic, 2 heads or 12 cloves
- ❑ Thyme, 8 large sprigs
- ❑ Small lemon, 1 for zest
- ❑ Extra-virgin olive oil, 3 cups
- ❑ Bay leaf, 1

dates stuffed with blue cheese mousse 55

SHOPPING LIST

- ❑ Blue cheese, 8 ounces. Select a sharp and fragrant blue cheese.
- ❑ Greek style unflavored yogurt, 4 ounces
- ❑ Medjool dates, 8 ounces (approximately 24 dates) You can usually find them in the dried fruit section of the supermarket.

parmesan crisps with goat cheese and chive mousse 56

SHOPPING LIST

- ❑ Goat cheese, 12 ounces
- ❑ Cream cheese, 6 ounces
- ❑ Chives, 2 ounces or 3 tablespoons
- ❑ Heavy cream, 3 tablespoons
- ❑ Finely shredded Parmesan cheese, 2 cups
- ❑ All-purpose flour, 2 teaspoons
- ❑ Fresh thyme, 3 sprigs

savory jam elephant ears (palmiers) 58

SHOPPING LIST

- ❑ Frozen puff pastry, one package that contains 2 sheets
- ❑ Jam*, 6 ounces
- ❑ Parmesan cheese, 3 ounces

tarragon chicken skewers with pistachio cream sauce   60

SHOPPING LIST

- Boneless skinless chicken breasts, two breasts, about 12 ounces
- Tarragon, 2 tablespoons chopped
- Lemon, 1 for juice
- Garlic, one clove
- Olive oil, 2 tablespoons
- Salt, healthy pinch
- Freshly ground pepper, ⅛ teaspoon
- Salt and pepper to taste

SAUCE

- Unsalted pistachio nuts, ¼ cup ground coarsely (use blender)
- Shallot, 1 chopped
- Olive oil, 2 tablespoons
- Heavy cream, ½ cup heavy cream
- Parmigiano Reggiano, ½ cup
- Salt, pepper and crushed red pepper to taste

balsamic chocolate truffles   62

SHOPPING LIST

- High quality dark chocolate, 8 ½ ounces chopped
- Cream, ¼ cup
- Pinch of salt
- Balsamic vinegar, 2 teaspoons
- Unsweetened cocoa powder, ¼ cup
- Confectioners' sugar, ¼ cup

THE INITIAL FLAME 66

pancetta wrapped shrimp with mustard wasabi dipping sauce 69

SHOPPING LIST

- Jumbo shrimp, 1 pound (size 10-15)
- Pancetta, 12 very thin slices
- Dijon mustard, 2 tablespoons
- Crème fraiche, 4 tablespoons (can substitute sour cream)
- Wasabi powder, 1 teaspoon
- Beer, 1 bottle of your favorite (optional)

goat cheese quesadillas with watermelon salsa 70

SHOPPING LIST

- 10-inch flour tortillas, 10
- Goat cheese, 10 ounces
- Lime, 1
- Lemon, 1
- Seedless watermelon, about ½ a medium size, enough to give you 2 cups of ½-inch cubes
- English cucumber, 1
- Red onion, 1 small
- Jalapeño peppers, 2
- Honey, 1 teaspoon
- Olive oil, ⅓ cup
- Fresh mint, a few sprigs

sake and miso marinated skirt steak salad 72

SHOPPING LIST

- Sake, 2 cups plus 1 tablespoon
- Red miso, 1 cup (found in Asian grocery stores)
- Vegetable oil, 1 cup
- Lemongrass, one 14-inch piece (optional)
- Garlic, 4 cloves
- Ginger powder, 2 teaspoons
- Skirt steak, 2 pounds
- Arugula, 6 cups (about 12 ounces)
- Romaine lettuce, 2 bunches
- English cucumbers, 2
- Cherry tomatoes, 1 pint (around 24)
- Kalamata olives or other brine-cured black olives, 2 cups. Buy ones that are pitted!
- Red onion, 1
- Mint, 4 sprigs 2 tablespoons
- Corn, 1 small can (15 ounces)
- Extra virgin Olive oil, 1 cup
- Sherry wine vinegar, 4 tablespoons
- Dijon mustard, 2 teaspoons
- Lemons, 2

grilled fruit and pound cake napoleon with berry sauce and tequila whipped cream   74

SHOPPING LIST

- Heavy cream, 1 cup
- 2 tablespoons of tequila (Silver or Blanco)
- 4 tablespoons of confectioners' (powdered) sugar
- Peaches, 6 (can substitute plums or nectarines)
- Bananas, 4
- Pound cake, 2
  You can use any brand easily found in your local supermarket.
- Mascarpone cheese, 8 ounces
- Jar of your favorite fruit preserves, 2 13-ounce jars
- Vegetable oil, ¾ cup
- Basil leaves for garnish

POOL PARTY 78

ultimate sangria 78

SHOPPING LIST

- ❏ Two bottles dry red wine
- ❏ ⅔ cup brandy
- ❏ 1 cup Cointreau or triple sec
- ❏ 1 cup pomegranate liquor (the secret weapon)
- ❏ 1 small lemon, thinly sliced crosswise
- ❏ 2 medium pear, diced
- ❏ 2 medium apples
- ❏ 1 cup of fresh berries such as raspberries, blueberries, etc.
- ❏ 12 ounces ginger ale

cold melon soup shooters with prosciutto salt 80

SHOPPING LIST

- ❏ Cantaloupes, 2 medium size
- ❏ Fruity white wine, like a Riesling or Chenin Blanc, 1 cup
- ❏ Honey, 1 tablespoon
- ❏ Lime, one for juice
- ❏ Nutmeg ¼ teaspoon
- ❏ Salt, ¼ teaspoon
- ❏ Cayenne, generous pinch
- ❏ Fresh mint, for garnish
- ❏ Prosciutto, 3 slices
  Ask the deli to slice the prosciutto slightly thicker than they usually do.
- ❏ Vegetable oil, 1 tablespoon

drunken pineapple rum shrimp ceviche 82

SHOPPING LIST

- ❏ Very fresh shrimp, 1 pound (31-40 size is a good size to use), shelled and deveined
- ❏ Limes, 2
- ❏ Orange juice, ½ cup
- ❏ Red bell pepper, 1
- ❏ Shallot, 1 medium
- ❏ Pineapple, 20 ounce can sliced
- ❏ Dark rum, 3 tablespoons
- ❏ Jalapeño peppers, 2
- ❏ Garlic, one clove minced
- ❏ Ginger powder, 1 tablespoon
- ❏ Fresh cilantro leaves, ¼ cup chopped
- ❏ Good quality extra-virgin olive oil, 2 tablespoons
- ❏ Salt, ½ tablespoon
- ❏ Tortilla chips

cobb salad sandwiches 84

SHOPPING LIST

- Avocados, 3 – they should be very ripe.*
- Blue cheese, 6 ounces - a nice assertive one like Roquefort works well
- Dijon mustard
- Bacon, 8 slices or about ½ pound
- Eggs, 4
- A loaf of good quality white bread, preferably unsliced or 4 rolls
- Whole skinless boneless chicken breasts, 2 (can substitute 1 pound of sliced turkey breast)
- Tomatoes, 2, sliced

lamb sliders with mint yogurt sauce and homemade pickled onions 86

SHOPPING LIST - PICKLED ONIONS

- Red onions, 2 large
- Red wine vinegar, 3 cups
- Olive oil, ¼ cup
- Sugar, 2 tablespoons
- Garlic, 2 cloves
- Whole black peppercorns, 6 (or ½ teaspoon of ground pepper)
- Fresh thyme, 4 sprigs
- Salt, 1 tablespoon

SHOPPING LIST - SLIDERS

- Plain Greek style yogurt, 1 cup
- Whole fresh mint, one bunch 1 cup loosely packed leaves plus 2 tablespoons minced
- Lemon, 1 small, juiced
- Ouzo 1 teaspoon (optional)
- Garlic, 1 clove, halved lengthwise
- Ground lamb, 1 ½ pounds
- Shallot, 1 medium
- Salt, ¾ teaspoon
- Black pepper, ½ teaspoon
- Ground allspice, ¼ teaspoon
- Olive oil, 2 ounces
- One loaf of thick French or Italian bread

7 TAILGATING IN STYLE 90

grilled vegetable antipasto with goat cheese on crostini 92

SHOPPING LIST

- ❏ Garlic, 2 cloves
- ❏ Balsamic vinegar, 3 tablespoons
- ❏ Red-wine vinegar, 2 tablespoons
- ❏ Dried basil, 1 teaspoon
- ❏ Dried oregano, 1 teaspoon
- ❏ Dried hot red pepper flakes, ¼ teaspoon
- ❏ Olive oil, ½ cup plus 2 tablespoons
- ❏ Vegetable oil, ½ cup
- ❏ Fennel bulbs, 2 small (about 1 ½ pounds)
- ❏ Red bell peppers, 3 medium size
- ❏ Large zucchinis or summer squash, 2 medium size
- ❏ Black or green brine-cured olives, ¾ pound
- ❏ Soppressata, ½ pound (can substitute salami)
- ❏ Goat cheese, 6 ounces
- ❏ Baguette, 1 each

chili rubbed beef tenderloin sliders with cilantro lime mayo 94

SHOPPING LIST

- ❏ Ancho chili powder, 1 ½ teaspoons
- ❏ Cayenne chili powder, 1 teaspoon
- ❏ Fine ground espresso coffee, 1 ½ teaspoons
- ❏ Brown sugar, 1 teaspoon
- ❏ Dry mustard, ¼ teaspoon
- ❏ Granulated garlic, 1 teaspoon
- ❏ Salt, 1 teaspoon
- ❏ Black pepper ½ teaspoon
- ❏ Center cut beef tenderloin, 3 pounds
- ❏ Small rolls, 20-24 (Silver dollar dinner rolls, mini-Hawaiian rolls or any soft crust small roll)
- ❏ Limes, 2 for juice
- ❏ Garlic, 2 cloves
- ❏ Hot sauce
- ❏ Dijon mustard, 1 teaspoon
- ❏ Cilantro, 1 bunch
- ❏ Mayonnaise, 1 cup
- ❏ Vegetable oil, 1 tablespoonS

roasted corn salad — 96

SHOPPING LIST

- ❏ Corn still in the husks, 8 ears
- ❏ Red bell pepper, 1
- ❏ Serrano peppers, 2
- ❏ Red onion, 1 small
- ❏ Fresh cilantro, 1 bunch
- ❏ Olive oil , ½ cup
- ❏ Garlic, 4 cloves
- ❏ Limes, 3 for juice
- ❏ Honey, 1 teaspoon
- ❏ Queso cotija cheese, ¼ pound (can substitute Feta cheese)

s'mores bars — 97

SHOPPING LIST

- ❏ Graham cracker crumbs, 2 ¼ cups (one box of crackers)
- ❏ Sugar, ⅓ cup
- ❏ Salt, ¼ teaspoon
- ❏ Butter, 1 stick (½ cup)
- ❏ Dark or bittersweet chocolate, 1 pound
- ❏ Mini-marshmallows, 4 cups

OCTOBERFEST 100
HOMEMADE BRATWURST PATTY SANDWICHES ON PRETZEL ROLLS 102

PRETZEL ROLLS SHOPPING LIST

- ❏ Active dry yeast, one small
- ❏ Sugar, 2 teaspoons
- ❏ All-purpose flour, 4 ½ cups
- ❏ Kosher salt, 2 teaspoons
- ❏ Butter, 4 Tablespoons
- ❏ Baking soda ¼ cup
- ❏ Egg, 1 large
- ❏ Large grain salt, like sea salt

SHOPPING LIST

- ❏ Ground pork, 2 ½ pounds
- ❏ Dried sage, 2 teaspoons
- ❏ Salt, 2 teaspoons
- ❏ Ground black pepper, 1 teaspoon
- ❏ Dry mustard, ½ teaspoon
- ❏ Nutmeg, ½ teaspoon
- ❏ Sugar, 1 teaspoon
- ❏ Worcestershire sauce, a few splashes
- ❏ Lager beer, 4 ounces
- ❏ Spicy German style mustard, a small jar
- ❏ Vegetable oil, 1 tablespoon

bratkartolffen (fried potatoes laced with bacon and onions) 105

SHOPPING LIST

- ❏ Potatoes 5 pounds – Yukon gold
- ❏ Bacon, 8 ounces
- ❏ Yellow onions, 2 (can substitute white onion or sweet onion)
- ❏ Vegetable oil, ½ cup
- ❏ Pepper, ½ teaspoon
- ❏ Salt, 1 teaspoon

schnitzel with baked apples stuffed with spicy red cabbage 106

SHOPPING LIST

- ❏ Veal cutlets, 1 pound (Veal is expensive; you may easily substitute chicken breasts or pork cutlets)
- ❏ All purpose flour, ½ cup
- ❏ Salt, ½ teaspoon
- ❏ Ground pepper, ½ teaspoon
- ❏ Bread crumbs, ½ cup
- ❏ Eggs, 2 large
- ❏ Oil for frying
- ❏ Lemon, 2 each

baked apples stuffed with spicy red cabbage — 108

SHOPPING LIST

- Extra-virgin olive oil, ¼ cup
- One head of red cabbage, 2 ½ to 3 pounds – cored and sliced ¼ inch thick
- Lemon, 1
- Red pepper flakes, pinch
- Red wine vinegar, ¼ cup
- Beer, ¼ cup
- Apples, 2 large – golden delicious or Cortland are good varieties to use.
- Butter, 2 tablespoons
- Cinnamon, 2 teaspoons

apple gingerbread bread pudding — 110

SHOPPING LIST

- All-purpose flour, 1¾ cups
- Baking powder, 1 teaspoon
- Baking soda, ¾ teaspoon
- Salt, ¼ teaspoon
- Ground ginger, 2 tablespoons
- Crystallized ginger, ⅓ cup (1 ¾ ounces)
- Ground cinnamon, 1 teaspoon
- Fresh ground nutmeg, ⅓ teaspoon
- Butter 4 ounces (1 stick)
- Dark brown sugar, ½ cup
- Honey, ¼ cup
- Eggs, 2 large
- Black strap molasses, 6 tablespoons
- Whole milk, ¾ cup
- Apple, 1 large (Jonagold, Braeburn, Golden Delicious, or Gala varieties are good choices)
- Whole milk, 2 cups
- Cream, ¾ cup
- Whole vanilla bean, 1 (can substitute 2 teaspoons of vanilla extract)
- Eggs, 3 large whole
- Egg yolks, 2 each
- Sugar, ½ cup
- Cinnamon, ½ teaspoon

COOKING WITH KIDDOS 114

dinosaur eggs 116

SHOPPING LIST

- Eggs, 4
- Carrot stick, 1
- Low fat mayonnaise, ⅓ cup
- Frozen peas, ¼ cup
- Iceberg lettuce, 4 large leaves

super crunchy fish sticks 117

SHOPPING LIST

- Canola oil cooking spray
- Grape-Nuts Cereal, 1 cup
- Whole-grain cereal flakes, 1 cup
- All-purpose flour, ½ cup
- Eggs, 2 large
- Tilapia fillets, 1 pound (Substitute any firm white flesh fish like Halibut or Orange Roughy)
- Your favorite prepared tartar sauce for dipping

mac 'n cheese 118

SHOPPING LIST

- Elbow macaroni, ½ pound
- Butter, 4 tablespoons
- Eggs, 2
- Evaporated milk, 6 ounces
- Dijon mustard, ½ teaspoon
- Sharp cheddar, 10 ounces shredded

violet's chocolate pudding 120

SHOPPING LIST

- Vanilla extract, 2 teaspoons
- Whole milk, 1 ½ cups
- Heavy cream, 1 ½ cups
- Sugar, 6 tablespoons
- Corn starch, 4 tablespoons
- Cocoa powder, 1 tablespoon unsweetened
- Bittersweet chocolate, 9 ounces (60-70% cocoa)
- Egg, 4 yolks
- Confectioners' sugar, 1 tablespoon (it is sometimes called powdered sugar)

10 DOUBLE DATE NIGHT 122

brie en croute and spinach salad 124

SHOPPING LIST

- ❏ Egg, 1 yolk only
- ❏ Frozen puff pastry, 1 sheet
- ❏ Brie, 1 small wheel approximately 3 ounces
- ❏ Apricot jam, 1 ½ tablespoons (can substitute any fruit jam that is not too sweet)
- ❏ Spinach, 4 ounces (about 6 cups)
- ❏ Dried blueberries, ½ cup (can substitute raisins)
- ❏ Raw pecans pieces, ½ cup unsalted
- ❏ Lemons, 2 for juice
- ❏ Olive oil, ½ cup

olive oil poached halibut with mint lemon pesto 126

SHOPPING LIST

- ❏ Olive oil, 4 ½ cups
- ❏ Garlic, 4 cloves
- ❏ Halibut, 4 (6-ounce) pieces with the skin and bones removed (Can substitute red snapper or cod)
- ❏ Lemon, 3
- ❏ Packed fresh mint leaves, 1 bunch
- ❏ Flat-leaf parsley, 1 bunch

fennel and spinach strudel 128

SHOPPING LIST

- ❏ Frozen chopped spinach, two 10-ounce packages
- ❏ Shallot, 1 each
- ❏ Fennel bulb, 1 small (sometimes called anise)
- ❏ Fennel seed, 2 teaspoons
- ❏ Ground nutmeg, ½ teaspoon
- ❏ Butter, 1 stick (½ cup)
- ❏ All-purpose or whole wheat flour, 2 tablespoons
- ❏ Ouzo or Richard, or other anise-flavored spirit, 2 tablespoons
- ❏ Grated Parmesan, 4 ounces
- ❏ One box of frozen phyllo sheets, you will need 6-8 sheets

pomegranate semifreddo with chocolate sauce 130

SHOPPING LIST

- ❏ Eggs, 2 large
- ❏ Sugar, ½ cup
- ❏ Pomegranate liqueur, 2 tablespoons
- ❏ Shelled and salted pistachio nuts, 6 ounces
- ❏ Heavy cream, 1 cup
- ❏ Bittersweet chocolate chips, 3 ounces

11 ROMANTIC DINNER (SPRING/SUMMER)   134

beet grapefruit salad   136

SHOPPING LIST

- Beets, 2 medium
- Grapefruits, 2 medium (they can be pink or red grapefruits)
- Sherry wine vinegar, 1 ½ tablespoons
- Dijon mustard, 1 teaspoon
- Extra-virgin olive oil, ½ cup
- Pre-washed mixed baby greens, a 5-ounce bag
- Avocado, 1 medium size and ripe
- Blue cheese, 1 ounce

chicken piperade over wasabi cauliflower puree   138

SHOPPING LIST

- Sherry vinegar, 3 tablespoons
- Skinless chicken breasts, ¾ pound boneless
- Butter, 2 tablespoons
- Onion, 1 small
- Red bell peppers, 1
- Garlic cloves, 3
- Cayenne pepper, ¼ teaspoon
- Cherry tomatoes, 4
- Ham, 2 ounces
- Watercress, 1 cup (Can substitute spinach) roughly chopped
- Cauliflower, 1 medium head
- Extra virgin olive oil, 2 to 3 tablespoons
- Light sour cream, 4 tablespoons
- Wasabi paste, 1 to 2 teaspoons, to taste

haricot verts with tarragon butter and black sesame seeds   140

SHOPPING LIST

- Sherry vinegar, 3 tablespoons
- Skinless chicken breasts, ¾ pound boneless
- Butter, 2 tablespoons
- Onion, 1 small
- Red bell peppers, 1
- Garlic cloves, 3
- Cayenne pepper, ¼ teaspoon
- Cherry tomatoes, 4
- Ham, 2 ounces
- Watercress, 1 cup (Can substitute spinach) roughly chopped
- Cauliflower, 1 medium head
- Extra virgin olive oil, 2 to 3 tablespoons
- Light sour cream, 4 tablespoons
- Wasabi paste, 1 to 2 teaspoons, to taste

white chocolate ginger mousse 141

SHOPPING LIST

- ❏ White chocolate, 4 ounces chopped (use a high quality one such as Lindt)
- ❏ Heavy cream, 5 ounces (a total of 11 tablespoons)
- ❏ Light corn syrup, 1 tablespoon
- ❏ Ground ginger, 2 teaspoons
- ❏ Confectioners' sugar, ¼ cup
- ❏ Berries for garnish, ½ cup (if available and in season, raspberries and blackberries)
- ❏ Dark chocolate for shavings as garnish (optional)

ROMANTIC DINNER ANOTHER NIGHT (FALL/WINTER) 144

farmers market grilled chopped salad with blood orange vinaigrette 146

SHOPPING LIST

- Broccoli, ½ head
- Brussels sprouts, 1 pint
- Parsnips, 1 medium
- Radicchio, ½ of one head (it looks like a small head of red lettuce)
- Vegetable oil, 2 tablespoons
- Coarse grain mustard, 1 rounded teaspoon
- Blood Orange vinegar, 2 tablespoons (Can substitute sherry vinegar)
- Extra-virgin olive oil, 5 tablespoons
- Tarragon (optional) 3 sprigs
- Shallot, 1 medium
- Feta cheese, 1 ounce

syrah braised and grilled short ribs on a bed of mascarpone jalapeño polenta 148

SHOPPING LIST

- Short ribs on the bone, 4 thick meaty pieces (2- 2.5 pounds)
- Bay leaf, 1
- Fresh thyme, 2 sprigs
- Vegetable oil, 1 tablespoon
- Bacon, ¼ pound
- Shallot, 1
- Carrot, 1
- Garlic, 2 cloves
- mushrooms, 4 ounces
- Syrah or other dry red wine, ¾ cups
- Beef broth, ½ cup
- Low sodium chicken stock, 32 ounces
- Butter. 4 ounces (1 stick)
- Yellow polenta, 9 ounces (250 grams)
- Mascarpone cheese, 3 ounces
- Jalapeño, 1 small

pomegranate glazed carrots 150

SHOPPING LIST

- Butter, 1 teaspoon
- Carrots, ½ pound
- Pomegranate juice, ½ cup
- Cinnamon stick, 1 (or 1 teaspoon of powder)
- Lemon, 1 small for zest

poached pears with dark chocolate sauce   151

SHOPPING LIST

- ❏ Pears, 2 small firm-ripe (preferably Bosc)
- ❏ White wine, 1 cup (Riesling or Viognier)
- ❏ Sugar, ¼ cup
- ❏ Cinnamon stick, 1 broken in half
- ❏ Bittersweet or semisweet chocolate, 4 ounces

BREAKFAST IN BED   154

brioche french toast stuffed with strawberries & cream   157

SHOPPING LIST

- Unsliced brioche or challah bread, ½ loaf
- Eggs, 2 large
- Heavy cream, 2 tablespoons
- Sugar, 1 teaspoon
- Vanilla extract, ½ teaspoon
- Butter, 3 tablespoons
- Cream cheese, 4 ounces
- Strawberries, ½ cup (if not in season, use frozen)
- Lemon, 1 for zest
- Honey, ½ teaspoon
- Maple syrup

ginger scones with peach bellini jam   158

SHOPPING LIST

- Frozen peaches, 2 pounds
- Sugar, 1 cup plus 2 tablespoons
- Lemon, 1 for juice
- Cornstarch, 2 tablespoons
- Sparkling wine, 4 tablespoons
- Egg, 1 large
- Heavy cream, ⅔ cup cold plus 2 tablespoons
- Flour, 2 cups
- Baking powder, 1 tablespoon
- Butter, 5 tablespoons
- Crystallized ginger, ¾ cup diced
- Raw sugar, 2 tablespoons (or sugar with large crystals)

low fat granola parfait   160

SHOPPING LIST

- Mixed organic whole grain flakes, 2 cups (look for a mix of oat, kamut, barley and wheat)
- Sliced almonds, ½ cup
- Butter, 2 tablespoons cold unsalted butter, cut into 6 pieces
- Whole wheat flour, 3 tablespoons
- Sugar, 1 tablespoon
- Cinnamon, ½ teaspoon
- Pure maple syrup, ¼ cup
- Honey, ¼ cup
- Vanilla extract, ½ teaspoon
- Dried blueberries, ¼ cup
- Dried cranberries, ¼ cup
- Plain yogurt, 1 cup
- Fresh seasonal berries, 1 cup (raspberries, blueberries, strawberries (hulled and sliced), and/or other fruit such as bananas or peaches sliced)

14 BRUNCH WITH THE IN-LAWS 164

bellini 165
SHOPPING LIST
- Peaches
- Champagne or prosecco

kir royale 165
SHOPPING LIST
- Chambord (can substitute any raspberry or black currant liqueur)
- Champagne

pumpkin muffins with brown sugar creme filling 166
SHOPPING LIST
- All purpose flour, 1 cup
- Baking powder, 1 teaspoon
- Baking soda, ¼ teaspoon
- Salt, ¼ teaspoon
- Ground cinnamon, ½ teaspoon
- Ground nutmeg, ¼ teaspoon
- Brown sugar, ¾ cup
- Canned pumpkin puree, ¾ cup
- Egg, 2 large
- Cream, ¼ cup
- Cream cheese, 4 ounces
- Vanilla extract, 1 teaspoon
- Chopped walnuts, ¼ cup

baked eggs with gruyere in prosciutto cups 168
SHOPPING LIST
- Prosciutto, 8 slices
- Egg, 4 large
- Gruyere, 2 ounces
- Fresh Spinach, 2 ounces
- Tomato, 1 large
- Garlic, 1 small clove
- Olive oil, 1 tablespoon
- Basil, 1 small bunch
- Chives, 1 small bunch

peaches in vanilla syrup over cinnamon yogurt 170
SHOPPING LIST
- Unflavored Greek yogurt, 1 ½ cups
- Cinnamon, ¼ teaspoon ground
- Dry white wine, ½ cup
- Water, ½ cup
- Sugar, ½ cup
- Vanilla bean, 1 (or 2 teaspoons of vanilla extract)
- Peaches, 4 medium size or ½ pound of frozen peaches
- Lemon, 1 for juice
- Pistachios, ½ cup

COCKTAIL PARTY FINGER FOOD 174

classic martini 175
SHOPPING LIST
- ❏ Gin (My personal favorites include Plymouth, Beefeater and Poodles)
- ❏ Dry Vermouth
- ❏ Stuffed olives (you can find olives stuffed with garlic, blue cheese, jalapeños besides the classic pimentos)

mojito 176
SHOPPING LIST
- ❏ Light rum
- ❏ fresh mint
- ❏ sugar
- ❏ sparkling water/ soda water
- ❏ fresh lime juice

death in the afternoon 176
SHOPPING LIST
- ❏ Absinthe
- ❏ Champagne

ginger scallops on wonton crisps with candied jalapeño 177
SHOPPING LIST
- ❏ Vegetable oil, 2 cups
- ❏ Large scallops, 12 halved horizontally
- ❏ Wondra Flour, ½ cup (also known as instant flour)
- ❏ Butter, ½ stick
- ❏ Ground ginger, 2 teaspoons
- ❏ Wonton skins, 25 (1 package)
- ❏ Jalapeño peppers, 3
- ❏ Sugar, ½ cup

crispy olives stuffed with chicken & feta sausage 178
SHOPPING LIST
- ❏ Ground chicken breast, 1 pound
- ❏ Feta, 6 ounces
- ❏ Dried sage, 1 tablespoon
- ❏ Garlic chili sauce, ½ teaspoon
- ❏ Spanish olives, 24 pitted large patted dry
- ❏ vegetable oil, 2 cups (for frying)
- ❏ All purpose flour, 1 cup
- ❏ Egg, 1
- ❏ Panko breadcrumbs, ½ cup

chipotle marshmallow crispy treats — 179

SHOPPING LIST

- Rice Krispies cereal, 6 cups
- Marshmallows, 10 ounce package
- Butter, 3 tablespoons
- Chipotle chili powder, 2 tablespoons
- Smoked paprika, 2 teaspoons
- Dried cranberries, ⅔ cup
- Salt, ½ teaspoon

miniature crab corn cakes with chive caper sauce — 180

SHOPPING LIST

- Mayonnaise, 1 ⅓ cups
- Eggs, 2 yolks
- Dijon mustard, 1 ½ tablespoons
- Lemon, 1 for juice
- Sriracha hot chili sauce, 1 teaspoon
- Dried tarragon, ¾ teaspoon
- Shallot, 1 large size
- Canned corn, 4 ounces (pure corn, not one with any seasoning or sauce)
- Blue crab finger crab meat, 1 pound (can substitute lump or jumbo lump crab)
- Panko, 1 ½ cups
- ½ cup of vegetable oil
- Fresh parsley, ¼ cup
- Chives, about 12-15 leaves (that is the long slender hollow blade)
- Lemon, 1 for juice
- Hot pepper sauce, ½ teaspoon
- Capers, 2 tablespoons

salmon in blankets with fried serrano cream — 182

SHOPPING LIST - CREAM

- Canola oil, 6 ounces
- Serrano chilies, 6 chilies
- White onion, one medium size
- A garlic clove
- Heavy cream, ½ cup

SHOPPING LIST

- Frozen puff pastry, 1 package with 2 sheets 17.3-ounce
- Salmon filets, 1 ½ pounds with the skin and pin bones removed.
- Shallots, 2
- Fresh tarragon, 4 stems (if you must, substitute 2 teaspoons of dried tarragon)
- Butter, 8 ounces

sweet potato, ham and leek frittata wedges with lemon aioli 184

SHOPPING LIST

- ❏ Butter, 4 tablespoons
- ❏ Sweet potatoes or yams, two medium size. about 1 ½ pounds
- ❏ Eggs, 8
- ❏ Hot sauce, a splash (use your favorite brand)
- ❏ Ham, 4 ounces (use any ham you like, just have the deli counter cut thick slices)
- ❏ Leek, 1
- ❏ Garlic, 3 cloves
- ❏ Chives, 1 small bunch
- ❏ Mayonnaise, ½ cup
- ❏ Olive oil, 1 tablespoon

tomato skewers with tequila vinaigrette 186

SHOPPING LIST

- ❏ Cherry tomatoes, 1 pint
- ❏ Avocados, 3 (they should be ripe but not mushy)
- ❏ Tequila, blanco, 1 ounce
- ❏ Grapefruit, 1 large
- ❏ Olive oil, 5 ounces
- ❏ Mint, 1 bunch
- ❏ Dijon mustard, 1 teaspoon

walnut, arugula and blue cheese crostini 188

SHOPPING LIST

- ❏ Butter, 8 ounces
- ❏ Baguette, 1
- ❏ Walnuts, 6 tablespoons
- ❏ Gorgonzola cheese, 3 ounces (you can substitute other blue cheeses)
- ❏ Olive oil, 1 tablespoon
- ❏ Honey, 1 teaspoon
- ❏ Arugula, 3 tablespoons
- ❏ Cherry tomatoes

white chocolate spice cookies — 190

SHOPPING LIST

- All-purpose flour, 2 cups
- Light brown sugar, ⅔ cup firmly packed
- Ground ginger, 1 teaspoon
- Fresh-ground pepper, ¾ teaspoon
- Baking soda, ½ teaspoon
- Unsweetened cocoa powder, ½ teaspoon
- Ground cinnamon, ¼ teaspoon
- Ground allspice, ½ teaspoon
- Salt, healthy pinch
- Butter, 1 cup (½ lb.) unsalted butter
- Vanilla extract, 1 teaspoon
- Lemon, 1 for zest
- White chocolate chips or pieces, 6 ounces
- Vegetable oil, 1 teaspoon
- Semi-sweet chocolate chips or pieces, 2 ounces

rum balls — 192

SHOPPING LIST

- Pecans, 1 ½ cups (can substitute hazelnuts, walnuts, or almonds)
- Vanilla wafer cookies, 1 ¼ cups (can substitute meringues, ginger cookies or chocolate wafers)
- Confectioners' sugar, 1 cup
- Unsweetened cocoa powder, 2 tablespoons
- Light corn syrup, 2 tablespoons
- Dark rum, ¼ cup (can substitute bourbon

POKER NIGHT WITH THE BOYS 196

Duck confit jalapeño poppers 198

SHOPPING LIST

- ❏ Freshly ground black pepper, ½ teaspoon
- ❏ Dried thyme, ½ teaspoon
- ❏ Bay leaf, 1
- ❏ Moulard duck legs, 4 (about 2 pounds total)
- ❏ Olive oil, 1 cup
- ❏ Salt, 1 teaspoon
- ❏ Grated parmesan cheese, 4 ounces
- ❏ Jalapeño peppers, 12

pumpkin seed crusted chicken bites with chipotle yogurt dipping sauce 200

SHOPPING LIST

- ❏ Greek style yogurt, 14 ounces
- ❏ Chipotle peppers in adobo sauce
- ❏ Lime, 1 each
- ❏ Honey, ½ teaspoon
- ❏ Raw unsalted pumpkin seeds, 2 cups (shelled)
- ❏ Ancho powder, 1 teaspoon
- ❏ Eggs, 2 large
- ❏ Fresh thyme, 1 teaspoon
- ❏ Salt, 1 teaspoon
- ❏ Chicken tenders, 2 pounds
- ❏ Extra-virgin olive oil, 2 tablespoons
- ❏ All Purpose flour, 2 cups

texas chili 202

SHOPPING LIST

- ❏ Bacon, ¼ pound (about 6 slices)
- ❏ Chuck steak or Brisket, 3 pounds
- ❏ Onions, 3 large ones
- ❏ Ground cumin, 1 tablespoon
- ❏ Ancho chili powder, 3 tablespoons
- ❏ Smoked paprika, 2 teaspoons
- ❏ Dried Mexican oregano, 1 teaspoon
- ❏ Ground black pepper, 1 teaspoon
- ❏ Dried thyme, ½ teaspoon
- ❏ Salt, ½ teaspoon
- ❏ Jalapeño pepper, 1 each
- ❏ One bottle of beer, preferably Shiner Bock
- ❏ Beef broth, 8 ounces
- ❏ Chopped tomatoes, one 28-ounce can
- ❏ Dried chipotle chilies, 2 each
- ❏ Corn starch, 1 tablespoon
- ❏ Carrots, 2 each
- ❏ Celery, 2 stalks
- ❏ Garlic, 6 cloves
- ❏ Olive oil, 2 tablespoons
- ❏ Bay leaf
- ❏ Grated cheddar cheese, 8 ounces
- ❏ Beans, one pound pinto or dried Yellow Indian Woman beans from www.ranchogordo.com

winners buttermilk pie 205

SHOPPING LIST

- ❏ Butter, ½ stick (¼ cup)
- ❏ Sugar, 1 cup
- ❏ Buttermilk, 1 ½ cups
- ❏ Eggs, 4
- ❏ All-purpose flour, 4 tablespoons
- ❏ Vanilla, 1 teaspoon
- ❏ Lemon, 1
- ❏ Salt, ¼ teaspoon
- ❏ Freshly grated nutmeg to taste
- ❏ Bourbon, ½ ounce
- ❏ Fresh seasonal berries, like raspberries or blueberries, 3 ounces
- ❏ Unbaked frozen 10-inch basic pie crust shell

about the author

CULINARY INSTRUCTOR DAVID HARAP has had a passion for food and cooking since he was a child. Working in commercial kitchens and catering halls to help put himself through Cornell University, David built a solid knowledge base of culinary fundamentals. His cooking style is very much influenced by his global travels and blends international culinary techniques with local and seasonal products. David teaches a wide range of classes, including many on entertaining, at the Central Market Cooking School and hosts an underground supper club, Austin Bite Club. He is also a partner and Global Practice Leader with Stanton Chase International, a leading global executive search firm.

order form

Fax orders: Fax this form to 425-984-7256.
Telephone orders: Call 925-838-9806.
                                                          Please have your credit card ready.
Email orders: orders@newyearpublishing.com
Postal orders by credit card or personal check:

                                                                 New Year Publishing, LLC
                                                                         PO Box 12793
                                                              Austin, TX 78711 USA

Name: _____

Address: _____

City: _____ **State/Zip:** _____

Telephone: _____ **Email:** _____

Quantity: _____ @ **$21.95 for** *Entertain Like a Gentleman*

Quantity: _____ @ **$29.95 for hardcover version of** *Entertain Like a Gentleman*

Quantity: _____ @ **$22.95 for** *Entertain Like a Texas Gentleman*

Bulk discounts are available. Call New Year Publishing for additional information.

Sales tax: Please add 9.25% for books shipped to California.
Shipping: $5.95 per book.
_____ **Total including applicable tax and shipping**

Payment: ____ Check   ____ Credit card

Card number: _____

Name on card: _____

Exp. date: _____

www.ingramcontent.com/pod-product-compliance
Lightning Source LLC
Chambersburg PA
CBHW081916170426
43200CB00014B/2741